A TRANSFORMATIVE JOURNEY OF MIDLIFE

Eve Sikora

The CRISIS Of The BEAUTIFUL AGE

Edition: Joanna Sosnowka
Translation: Maria Pogwizd
Cover and graphic design: Malgorzata Sokolowska
Illustrations: Anna Gajowniczek
Text Compostion: InkWander

ISBN: 9788396928122

Limitless Mind Publishing Ltd
15 Carleton Road
Chichester
PO19 3NX
England
Tel. +44 7747761146
Email: office@limitlessmindpublishing.com

Dear Reader!

*Find us on **Facebook/Instagram**:*
limitless mind publishing

*And visit our page on **Amazon***
by entering: limitless mind publishing into the search bar
or by scanning the QR code to see our other titles.

♥ *We would greatly appreciate your opinion. It means a lot to us.*

For the closest person to my heart
- for myself

My letter to you

I decided to write a letter to you – a letter to a woman. This whole book is a form of a letter. I felt it'd be easier for me to tell you all of this that way. So Dear Woman, I'm writing this letter to you. I'm writing about myself and my experience on working with people. I will mix my private life with a professional one, because in my case they always go together. It's impossible to do it otherwise. You can't be a therapist, and not be a human being. That's a great challenge: to be a therapist and do good in a private life. Some people think it's easier for a therapist, because they mastered their minds and feelings. Nothing further from the truth. Being a therapist and a human being, usually is way harder than being just a human being. Maybe I writing to you, a therapist – woman?

This letter is being written by a simple woman, mother to three sons; no longer a wife, just a woman. This letter is being written by a woman who has similar problems to yours. Maybe I'm one step further on the self-discovery journey. But there still are hard moments that I can't overcome. I don't know if they are slowly vanishing or becoming less painful, maybe I gain some hope for things heading the right direction. I know this is a never-ending journey. I (unfortunately) don't have all the life wisdom, but I believe I still have something to offer. I don't fall apart every time life wants to test me. I'm unbreakable. I'm strong and capable. And that feels new, that's why I decided to write this letter to you. I thought you'd like to feel the same way. I want you to feel complete, internally coherent, strong. So complete that I lack nothing. I have a handful of comforting thoughts; I have ideas for action; I have faith in people; I have a lot of life energy and I still look at the world cheerfully.

If I manage to make you feel even for a moment that you are not alone, that there is someone else who thinks and feels like you, this will be my reward for the effort I put into writing these words. I felt a mission to be useful to someone with all my mind, creative outlook and way of being. A mission to be of use to you. And of course, I won't tell you what to do with your life, but maybe I can inspire you to start living your life to the fullest.

I wrote this letter while I was in crisis and I started coming out of it. I helped myself by writing this. At first I wrote only to me, then I thought, that maybe it will be useful to someone, because what I feel is universal. I decided to write down my ideas. First came the titles of the chapters that multiplied in my head, I didn't know where they came from and I just wrote them down. When my close friends came to me, I read them the titles, and they said in unison: Write! You must write it! It's important what you have to say! Women need it! And, probably on the second day after that meeting, I started writing. It was amazing. It was writing itself. My thoughts formulated itself.

I wrote every day for one month. It felt like I was in a trance. As I wrote, I went through the entire lunar cycle. I wrote to you with all my heart. Sometimes I would go to bed not knowing what I would write about the next day, and wake up in the morning inspired by a dream or an idea. Sometimes I would wake up in the night and write down some important thoughts or ideas for the next chapters. It cannot be described. I felt like a medium, like an intermediary. I felt I had to write and I knew what. Such flow in full release. Of course, I had a lot of fun and excitement. In the meantime, life went on as normal - going to work, taking care of the children, house, etc.

I did some work for myself. I discovered many important areas. I went through tasks that I also proposed to you. I went through my Crisis of the Beautiful Age, and now I propose to go the same path for you.

I never liked the name: midlife crisis, so I created a new one, my own, more friendly in reception. Hence the title of the book The Crisis of the Beautiful Age. Maybe it will even turn out to be an interesting idea to change this term for a better one. This book isn't just for women in a midlife crisis. It is for women who are going through any kind of crisis; lost in life; need some major life change.

Age doesn't make any difference here. This is a book for women who have ups and downs in life. It is also a "preventive" book, it prevents serious mental problems when crises occur. Because crises affect everyone, but not everyone comes out of them unscathed. It can also be a book for men who want to get to know the world of the female psyche, and maybe also use something for themselves. I invite you too!

There are moments in the book where it is worth stopping and doing the task. They can be done in a regular notebook or in a notebook specially prepared by me. I called it Anti-Crisis Workbook. If you want to use it, I have included links to all tasks (footnotes) in the text. I suggest doing these tasks on a regular basis while reading the book.

You can also do these tasks after reading the whole thing (and here, I warn you, it can be more difficult, because it is not easy to return to something that has already ended). The choice is yours. You can also not do the tasks and come back to the book when you need it more (for example, in some difficult moment in your life, which is yet to come). Of course, I do not wish anyone to have a crisis, but I know life and unfortunately I know that life difficulties are quite common and happen to everyone, to a greater or lesser extent.

I wish you a good reading and fruitful work!

And if you would like to see and listen to me, please visit my YouTube channel: Sikorka Flow. There I talk about life and share how I think and feel.

Good Luck

The Crisis of the Beautiful Age

I don't really like this name: midlife crisis – it doesn't sound good. It's sounds like a name of a disease, like there's something wrong with you. You got it – you are a clinker. You shouldn't get it. You should go through life without feeling it – the midlife crisis is bad!

Meanwhile men exchange wives for younger ones or cars for more expensive ones. They start running as if they want to pass their time, catch up with their youth. People laugh at such men. Women start going to the gym, do plastic surgery, look for lovers (also younger ones?), get lazy, get fat, lose weight, complain more, cry because they want to be younger and more beautiful. The world laughs at such women. That's why nobody wants to have a midlife crisis because it's a failure, because it's...

Well, what to tell the world? That it got to me, and I used to laugh at such people? That I don't know what's going on with me, but I guess that's it? How does it sound?! Who can advise me here? What's the advice here? Who knows? What's the advice here? How to get through such a crisis? And is it really him???

Have you had a crisis at all?

I called it the Crisis of the Beautiful Age. The name appeared in my head out of anger at the previous term and as a response to what I should call something that is happening to me.

Crisis is a difficult time. A time of change, challenges, difficulties and hope.

Age - everyone is getting older, every day, everyone gets it, time, passing, gaining years (and wisdom too?)

Beauty - this is the time of searching for the beauty of this world, yourself and this unique time that passes. It is an attempt to stop the moment, to appreciate what is.

The Crisis of the Beautiful Age is a time of losing the meaning of life and the idea for yourself. It is a time of searching for a way (often a new one) into oneself. The Crisis of the Beautiful Age is a difficult time of searching for beauty. It's time to stop and look within yourself. It's consent to change. It's a painful time. It's a beautiful time. The Crisis of the Beautiful Age is an existential crisis, a crisis of the meaning of life so far, the vision of the future and the meaning of life in general.

However, maybe you don't have a Crisis of the Beautiful Age? Maybe you're having a midlife crisis? Some kind of crisis? You have a serious problem and you are not quite young? As he called, so he called. You come out of crises, crises may be needed.

I am a woman, you are a woman. Shall we talk about the Crisis of the Beautiful Age in Women's lives?

When Life Starts To Suck

It starts with pain. The pain was from the very beginning. Seemingly ridiculous ... But, is a labor pain ridiculous? I'm not the one to judge, but I know it is. There's pain in my soul. But I wouldn't exist without it.

A normal life, the one that used to make me happy, suddenly started to cause pain. But a lot came from that pain, exactly as it is with a labor pain......... but I've noticed it way to late. Now I see the sense in pain, but before I couldn't see it at all. I was crying and didn't really know why. Okay, sometimes I knew. A chaos sought into my life.

I started to hate the world I'd been intricately creating before. The lifestyle I've been leading for the past twenty years is no longer to my liking. I stopped enjoying what I used to enjoy; I stopped loving what I used to love.

I was reborn from this pain. Now I know that and I am grateful for it. I hope that from your pain you will be born.

Nobody told me what was wrong with me. When I said I had a midlife crisis, my friends looked at me strangely. Their eyes were so big, they smiled slightly, sometimes almost imperceptibly or with embarrassment. They heard a phrase that didn't seem to mean much to them either. They were smiling, maybe at the vision of the man in their head, the one with the younger woman and the younger car. They didn't know what to say. Because what does it mean for a woman to have a midlife crisis? Who knows that? How does she really show up? How to treat it? I have not found a book about such a crisis in women.

I read dozens of books about crisis, psychology and life, and from that I conjured up a new me. There's no book about it? Amazing! I thought I would share with you what I experienced, maybe it will be a helpful story for you. Can I be an inspiration for you? I know your story is different, your problems are about different things. It is possible that together we will capture their essence ...

Shall we talk about our beautiful crisis?

Maybe you are at the beginning of the road, maybe in the process... It's not beautiful with you too? I'm already elsewhere. Already, from a slightly different perspective, I look at my experiences, which is why I have the courage to write to you.

In part, it will be a summary of the knowledge acquired, with tips on where to look for it and explore it. In part it will be my story from my own today's perspective (plus notes from that painful time), and in part it will be about you, a modern woman who struggles with herself, who searches, asks, has her needs, waits, suffers , thinks…

When Someone Writes…
…a Letter to You

My dear lost Woman! I'm writing this letter to you in a form of a book. I'm just like you. We are cut from the same cloth. We have the same structure, the same brain functionality, the same hormones. Maybe slightly different shapes, maybe slightly different hair. We live in the same world. We were both born on this Earth in modern times. In times of complete information chaos, great distance from nature. In times of uncertainty, processed food, television, the Internet, cars, planes and big cities. We are so tiny in this whole world, so fragile and vulnerable. I am writing you this letter to make you feel that you are not alone... to know that you always have yourself!

Hey, I'm Eve. Eve as eve, a day before something big. I was even born as if on the eve, exactly at 0:00. I got a good one! I am as special and unrepeatable as Christmas Eve. I was born to live. Maybe for something else? Maybe to write you a letter? Am I still here for something? I discover the answer to this question every day. Sometimes I'm alive and I don't even remember that I'm alive, that I am. And yet I am. So are you. You are! We're! Did you already know that you are also unique and unrepeatable? No? Nobody told you that? Hi hi hi… Think about it.

No one has to tell you that, after all, you are one you, there is no other like you. You are inimitable, you cannot be compared to anything. You are unique and original - even if you don't know it.

If you are reading these words, you are probably a woman who has lost her way. A woman in crisis; who seeks answers to her questions, a woman who suffers. You're probably over 30 or in your 40s, maybe younger. In fact, the exact age does not matter here, because the Crisis of the Beautiful Age could have gripped you earlier, because you like to be aware, because you think, because you anticipate the facts in your mind. You can also be much older and you are struggling with something - for example, with the fact that you have a crisis that has not been resolved for several or several decades and you carry great, long-hidden pain. In any case, you are certainly at the most appropriate age for yourself, which is beautiful!

If you are a woman who has drowned out herself, her pain, her crisis with alcohol, drugs or other addiction for some time, start with addiction therapy, because this is the most important thing now. Then there will be time for everything else - put this book down and come back to it sober and healed. It will be waiting for you as a reward for your hard work while recovering from addiction. Now there is no point in reading it, because being in active addiction will only make your situation worse, and the content contained in it will deepen your pain. If you are a partner of an actively addicted person - then also deal with this problem first. If in your childhood you experienced a lot of very difficult things, traumas - go to a therapist first.

If you are a man interested in the inner world of women, you want to feel it, understand it better or want to help your woman in difficult struggles - then read on, I invite you. Maybe you will find something valuable here. I hope that I also write for men and in a language that you understand. Because in fact and in fact, we are very similar to each other!

When You Almost Came Up Against a Brick Wall

Do you feel like you are in a situation that doesn't have a good solution? Like there's nothing more waiting? You hit this brick wall with your head and nothing? Oy, your head hurts! Does it sometimes hurt way to much? Do you have migraines?

It may be a sign that you are in an inner prison, that you have locked yourself from the inside and are yanking at the cage door. Did you have a key and lost it? You didn't and you don't? Someone stole from you? No key? Is there a combination lock? Don't know the code? Damn!

Attention! The key is in your heart! Seriously! At the bottom, maybe somewhere very deep. You have to get in there or infiltrate it somehow and get it. Otherwise you won't leave.

No one will tell you what to do, no one will solve the mystery of your life for you. It's such a life escape room with a great task of finding the key and getting out. Okay, in some tasks you will be able to help yourself with hints from relatives or friends. In some tasks, the support of specialists is acceptable. Your head is the most important. So note any clues that come your way so you don't miss anything important. Where to take notes?

When You Buy a Notebook, to put on paper what's in your head

Dear! Buy yourself a beautiful notebook! Choose the prettiest of all! Just yours, just purposely for you. That's a place where you can write down all your thoughts. No one will ever read it. Make it your dairy, sketchbook. Make it your safe space. With this notebook help you will communicate with yourself. There you will write questions, discoveries, experiences, answers that will lead you to find the most important code for your exit door from the crisis.

I also created a special notebook with tasks: Anti-Crisis Workbook. It is synchronized with the book/letter you are reading. It is available in the same place where you bought this book. However, if you experience any difficulties in acquiring the issue, you can contact me or search for information about purchasing (both the issue and my other publications). You will find my contact information at the end of the text, just before the acknowledgments.

It's like going back to school. You write, and the mind knows that what you write is important. He learned it at school. Write - it makes more sense than you think. This is super important. Much of what you write will amaze you, surprise you. Chaotic thoughts are difficult to express through language. It is only when put on paper that they form words, gain meaning, make sense and create greater order, greater clarity. Plus, you'll have a document of your own work, a map of your own head, and a better chance of getting to the code. Just because you don't know the code doesn't mean it doesn't exist. It won't be easy - work hard and you'll see results. It took me less than 4 years! Maybe you'll go faster! You have more tips. Be patient. Go at your own pace.

My notebook is next to me. I write my thoughts in it. He is my support and I can tell him anything! I open to a random page and read. Fuck! I have that everything! What I mean? Even my therapist doesn't know what I mean. Recently, I left her bitter. She said that my problems are caused by some characteristic of me. Yes, that's what I was afraid of, something was wrong with me. There's something! I am complete, fit, I have arms, legs, mind. I gave birth to three healthy children. I have a smart, loving husband. I have the profession I wanted, the education I dreamed of, I have living parents, a wonderful sister. I have myself, I am aware, I have courage, I have a desire to develop, I have finally found my passion and I have a lot of ideas for myself. I have a growing business. I have a house, a car, my room, my computer with Photoshop. I have a friend in Poland and a friend in England. I have lots of wonderful women around. I have a gift for finding good people. I have dreams! I have no peace. I have no joy. I have no consent to passing and consent to my changing body. I'm mentally unstable.

I'm like a little girl in the body of a 43-year-old woman. I feel like a girl, sad and abandoned, misunderstood, neglected. And in the mirror I see wrinkles, smaller and smaller eyes. I see an old woman. Something's not right here. Connection is missing. A girl or a woman? Child or mother? Ending or beginning life? Nice or pissed off? Smiling and sad? What's this all about? any riddle? find the key? Go through the maze? Connect the dots? Okay, I'm taking up the challenge - the task of life. I'm a therapist! Psychologist. I help people find their way back to themselves, and meanwhile I've lost mine. What an irony! I look around me and I don't see anything cool. There's a wall in front of me. There is emptiness in me, fear and bitterness in my belly. Tension on the face. I know it. Me and the wall. Myself.

Would you believe I really opened my notebook to a random page? I can't believe it myself. This often happens when I listen to myself, some magic happens. There are no words to describe it, but you probably understand me. You probably know these amazing coincidences and cases. Do you know your inner voice? Are you listening to him or are you ignoring him? do you like each other? I can't tear myself away from writing, because inspiration is flying, and it's already 1:49 at night. I will listen to the voice of reason and go to sleep, because tomorrow the youngest will wake up at 7:30 in the morning and call: Mom, when is breakfast? Sometimes you have to ignore your inner voice, which is a pity...

He woke up at 9.30 - amazing, how did he know that he needed to sleep longer today? Thanks, son!

When in the same time gets you: mid-life Crisis, existential crisis, empty nest crisis, marital crisis, identity crisis – you can be sure something wrong is happening

Crisis – as dictionary says: *Crisis – an internal experience of confusion and anxiety to the degree that formerly successful coping mechanisms fail us and ineffective decisions and behaviors take their place.*

Exactly – confusion and anxiety.

Roland Kachler in his book *Overcome the Crisis* describes: *the verbs krino, krinein mean to divide, disconnect, separate. They, in turn, derive from the root, which means "to cut, to cut". According to the original sense, a crisis is therefore a place of cutting, in which a person's previous life breaks and threatens to break up. As a cut divides in two halves, so the scar of the crisis runs in the place where good and evil meet in life, and it is not known which side will prevail. In medicine, the concept of crisis is used in the same sense: it means the apogee and breakthrough in the course of the disease, aimed at improving or worsening the patient's health. or let them win. So a crisis is also a struggle between two forces. In life crises, old desires and wishes that strive to maintain the status quo "fight" with those that strive for change. Although it is during crises that a person clings to the old personality structures that have provided security so far, a difficult situation forces him to develop new elements of his "I". In Chinese, the words "danger" and "opportunity" are expressed with the same symbol.*

A crisis is both: it is both the danger of having to deal with a difficult life situation that becomes a source of suffering, and the chan-

ce for a new beginning and personal maturation. The maturation and psychological development of a person do not run only in a straight line - sometimes it breaks down or jumps sharply. One can venture to say that the true maturation of the personality takes place only in and through crises.[1]

It may be that you have more crises at once. For me, it just happened that one crisis resulted from another and they combined into a great combo, or maybe the Crisis of the Beautiful Age, which can have different faces. For you it may be something else. Maybe you struggle more with your mind than with the reality around you? Or maybe it is reality that overwhelms you and relationships with loved ones make life difficult? Maybe you no longer like the life you've been leading for years? Maybe something that you used to have the strength to deal with has started to bother you? Maybe you need to drive less? Maybe you need less excitement? Or maybe you need more experience? Maybe the pressure of time stresses you out and you see that you will not achieve everything in life? You realize that you won't read all the good books, you won't watch all the recommended and cool movies waiting for you. You see that time doesn't have as much as it used to, that it somehow goes faster and the days pass faster. It used to be slower. Is time speeding up for you? Can it slow down? Maybe now you're starting to get bored with what you have? Maybe the day passes on monotonous, uninteresting activities and you just wait for the evening to go to sleep? If you have children, you see how fast they grow. Maybe yours will soon leave the nest, maybe they have already left? Maybe they are a few years old, but you are aware that it is only a moment… they have only just been born… What will you do with yourself when they go their separate ways? Have an idea for yourself? Can you imagine yourself without children? Can you imagine yourself and your husband alone? What will you do? Will you be interested? Maybe you're wondering if you want to grow old with this man? Do you want to see him get older? Maybe you're a pretty good match for each other and that's off topic, just that you won't know how to spend your time. Or maybe you know what you want and you lack the courage to do it? Maybe everyone dissuades you from your ideas, blocks your youthful

---

[1] A fragment o Roland's Kachler's book „*Pokonaj Kryzys*" from 2012, used as quotation in version from 31.02.2020. Can be found in Polish version online: https://opoka.org.pl/biblioteka/T/TS/wam_2012_pokonaj_kryzys_

enthusiasm to do something new, maybe something crazy? Does it feel like your last call? Your last life chance?

Write down everything that is bothering you in your notebook. Do it honestly! Remember, no one will read this. These are notes for you, this is your honest conversation with yourself. Describe and face what bothers you, what comes to your mind, what stubbornly comes back to your mind and what you try to deny, pretend that it doesn't exist. If it is, it is. See it, take it out, watch it! Describe it![1]

If you are reading these words, it may mean that you have been struggling with the crisis for a long time. Maybe you didn't even know it was a crisis. Maybe you thought something was wrong with you? did I guess? It's standard! If something doesn't go our way, the first reaction appears quickly - something is wrong with me! You've probably been struggling with this unnamed condition for a long time and you don't know what to do with yourself, you don't know to whom and what to say. You are afraid of people's reactions. Or have you already tasted some of the reactions? Oh come on, it'll pass! Don't be silly! Don't overdo it! Give yourself time, go to a psychiatrist and so on... If you've been struggling with yourself and suffering for some time, now I suggest you take action and take a slightly different approach to the matter. Name your crisis You can name it a word, a sentence, maybe several crises – capture it in your words. Write it down in your notebook.

In my flowery notebook I wrote one day: *I was calm today. Every hour more and more calm, more and more at home. I am starting to accept that I am going through a crisis, I am starting to allow myself to experience difficult feelings without reproaching myself, with greater acceptance of myself and my story. I don't argue with it (with the crisis), I don't struggle - I accept it and I become calmer. I start to listen to what He wants to tell me, I start to listen to myself - what my inner forces want to tell me. I can hear the desire to change. I hear longing, regret for the past, hope for the future. I want to take care of myself, I want to take care of myself, cuddle up, talk to myself. I haven't done that before.[2]*

---

[1] exercise 1
[2] exercise 2

When it hurts so damn much

The mental pain is as painful as a toothache. We need to do something about it. It tells us about something. You go to the dentist with your tooth and ask him to drill it out, clean it, and then seal it. You trust that he will do it right and you expect pain. You know it's gonna hurt. You can ask for anesthesia, but you know that this is interference in you, in your tooth, in your body and you agree to it. After you pay, you leave relieved. And you think: now I will brush my teeth more carefully!

Mental pain is like a toothache. Pain tells you something is breaking. Like a tooth. It won't stop hurting itself. Maybe it will quiet down a bit for a while, but then it will come back again, maybe even stronger. Mental pain requires professional intervention. Will you trust someone like a dentist and go with your head? Will you ask him to *ream it, to open it?* Will you accept the pain and intimacy of an embarrassing situation? At the dentist you open your mouth - and at the therapist you open your soul. One visit is not enough (root canal treatment may be needed). Matters accumulated over the years, hidden secrets, unspeakable difficulties will require more time, more painful visits. After some time, you have a chance to feel relief. This is my next offer for you. Go with you to someone wise, take your head, your thoughts, your feelings there. It's not a shame to take care of your mental health, it's not a shame to take care of your brain. You would go with the liver, with the eye, the ear, with the leg too. I guess it's better than doing nothing? Already have a notebook? Now call a brain specialist.

After my first visit during the crisis, I wrote: First visit to Mrs. Anne. I cried the entire meeting. I told you about what I've been through recently, how I feel. There were so many tears. I felt like a little girl - but respectfully listened to and as if hugged (by a good mother). I cried for an hour after the meeting. Now I am calm, peaceful.

You already have two specific clues. Are we going further? You want more? Act, don't stand still. Idleness can be very damaging at times.

If you like the task that I will propose, please stop reading this text for a moment and complete the task. Give yourself time to cool down, think, write down. You might need a few hours, maybe a few days. You do not have to rush. You can treat this letter as a suggestion of specific moves that you can perform at your own pace ... Take your time. You'd better be acting, not just reading. This is my idea for our cooperation. I will give you tasty morsels, and you will eat them quickly or savor them. You can complete tasks and start to change something, or you can just read about them and probably forget about them right away. A task that has only been read is not counted as completed, and the change will not occur spontaneously.

My words can be your companion on the journey towards female maturity. And it's not about adulthood (although you can reach it in the meantime)), but it's about becoming a mature woman. Ripe like a fruit, sweet and full of flavor for others. Maturity is wisdom, mindfulness, calmness. What does maturity mean to you? What kind of woman do you want to become?[1]

---

[1] exercise 3 and 4

Stop being so hard on yourself

Hey, I spent the entire day in the office. I had many interesting meetings with women. A few ideas came up that would like to exist here. I came home thinking that I would continue writing, but somehow I'm not doing well today. I know, I should rest and sleep well, then get back to writing. I'm probably like you - it's hard for me to let go and it's even harder to rest. That's why I'm good at doing too much! You too? Let's continue it tomorrow, because today I will take care of myself and go to sleep. Bye!

I slept well and when I woke up I walked around the house. I ate buckwheat bread with tomatoes and arugula, which I baked myself. I drank coffee with oat milk. I talked to my friend about her renovation and the fun of arranging the interior of a new apartment. And I've been working on not blaming myself for doing nothing. It even worked. I sat down to write at 1 p.m. and the world didn't collapse, and I'm so much more open to action now.

Do you also feel that it is difficult for you to rest, that it is difficult for you to let go of work, that you feel that you are doing something wrong when you do nothing? In our culture, women are under pressure to act. We women learn from an early age that if we do nothing, we are not valuable. We are afraid of the word lazy. Because if someone said or thought that about us, it would be very unpleasant for us. We learn to be robots - that is, the one that does. Even when he has free time, he does something: cleans, cooks, irons, takes care of the children, catches up with work, maybe sews, draws, creates something. Only when you do something worthwhile do you feel valuable? Can you do nothing, sit in an armchair and look at the wall, at the window, at yourself? Can you lie on the floor and think about nothing? Can you lie in the bathtub without a phone and enjoy the silence when the children are asleep (or when you don't have children because you simply don't have any, or they are at grandma's or dad's house)? Can you just be and do nothing? Just be?

You know women who take too much on their shoulders and then complain to the world that they are so tired, that they are so used that they do not have time for themselves? Sure you know! Or are you one of them? Nobody teaches us to rest, they don't talk about it at school, mom doesn't talk about it, it's not a popular and important topic. They teach us how to work, they teach us how to drive, how not to take care of ourselves, how to be efficient and useful.

You may think that when you rest, you are not useful, that it has no value and sense, you are even selfish! really? Is a person who does not rest really more efficient, lives longer and does good? Not necessarily, especially if then she still has a grudge against the world that he drove her. We often have a grudge against our mothers that they stop by, that they don't think about themselves, that they do too much for their strength and feel exhausted. One would like to say: Why are you doing this? Does anyone expect this from you? You make this job yourself. You could rest or go on a trip, finally do something for yourself, not for someone else.

I believe that a woman is not a robot! It's not designed to run at 100% all the time. The nature of a woman is different. A woman is changeable, she has ebbs and flows of strength. When he allows himself to rest properly, he is then able to work properly. I think you should pay attention to your nature, to your natural processes. In this way, you can respect yourself more and use your abilities better. Don't you think that when you get a good night's sleep, you have more energy afterwards? If you allow yourself days of stagnation, then days of activity come with great force. Yes Sir. Rest makes a lot of sense! I work with women in such a way that they understand it and put it into practice. And this is a big and very difficult task in the therapy process. Who would have thought? An important task in therapy - learning to rest. It sounds trivial, but it is not trivial, because it is strongly connected with learning to take care of yourself, i.e. with the *Great Task in the Crisis of the Beautiful Age.*

You know, I suspect that you have a lot of lagging behind in rest, that many of your last years or months were a period in which you did not have much time for yourself. I gave birth to three sons, each 7 years apart. Years in diapers... Although I still had only one small child, I feel that my life was a great commitment to family life, a great struggle for a sense of security, for existence, for development. And I don't deny that I've been a housewife for the last twenty-two years.

Maybe just a hen, but it was enough to make me tired. Was I right to be tired? Did I ever have the right to be fed up with everything? Did I have the right to have a lot of fear that I would not be able to handle this life of mine, that I was not a good mother, wife, partner? Did I have the right to get lost and get lost? Was I right to lose myself in this? Yes! I had the right, and unfortunately I used that right beautifully.

If you have years, not months, of catching up on rest - you will have a lot of work with it. By the way, it can be enjoyable if you allow yourself to. Count how many years you have been driving and calculate how much rest you need hi hi hi ... How to calculate it? Well, you can't. Somehow, you have to recalculate it in your head. In a moment you will know that it was a lot and a lot of rest is needed. Women in the Crisis of the Beautiful Age are usually well-fed, very tired, neglected women (not necessarily externally - they can be beautiful and slim and have nice coats, dresses and earrings). However, they are so neglected internally. Have you taken good care of yourself in recent years? Did you really do what you wanted, lived how you wanted, pursued your bold ideas, pursued your dreams? Or maybe you were waiting for someone to take care of you and then you cured yourself and you didn't wait anymore, but inside you was waiting and ... shit ... Well, I'm kidding, but how do we wait for the world to take care of us We probably won't get it. did you wait? Waiting makes all the sweetness in us bitter. I didn't wait. And finally, I took matters into my own hands.[1]

Today, for example, I bought red tulips and I look at them sometimes, how they are standing in a glass. And they are looking at me. And today I decided not to wait for someone to buy them for me. I'm also wearing a red blouse, I have red blood and I'm a heavy sleeper and I'm not waiting anymore.

Do an experiment. Turn off all media and sit comfortably in silence for about fifteen minutes. Some people have a big problem with this task. Disabling all media jammers directs you to what you want to jam. Sometimes there is fear, sometimes painful memories, sometimes difficult current relationships. Try to stop jamming yourself, for a while (including work) to listen to what is important in you. It can hurt.[2]

And then you can take a piece of paper or a beautiful notebook and write a letter to yourself.[3]

---

[1] exercise 5
[2] exercise 6
[3] exercise 7

When you write a letter to yourself

Yes, it might sound weird. You haven't written anything in a while? You have never wrote a letter to yourself? Hi hi hi… Then maybe give it a try and see what will happen.

One day I wrote:

Dear Eve!

I am writing you this letter because I know that you are going through a difficult time in your life right now.

I always thought of you as a brave girl, who was doing great in life. You were a model of a happy, fulfilled woman for me (and for many other women too). I know you didn't feel it fully. You were always chasing something. You were looking for something, you still felt unsatisfied. You've been very lucky in your life. Your dreams came true, you kept pushing forward and achieving your goals. I have always been amazed by your energy and wondered where you get all the strength from. I was happy to see how happy you were with your husband, how in love you were with him and how loved by him.

You have reached a very difficult time in your life. You are 43 years old and you are thinking about the future. You wonder how you would like to spend it and with whom. You are experiencing huge dilemmas related to your marriage, which was wonderful until recently. For some time now you have felt lonely, misunderstood, neglected, overlooked and unloved in this relationship. You have increasingly difficult feelings for your husband. Alone, you don't show him good feelings … You feel that he has little really nice things for you except the love he professes, and you don't feel it. You crave affection, intimacy, exchange, community. You want more. You have lived a good life together, but now this life is a clumsy continuation for you.

Write an honest letter to yourself from the bottom of your heart. Check what you have to say to yourself.

When you buy yourself a gift

Let's start with little things. You already have a notebook. You already have flowers for yourself (at least planned)? Look around and think about what could bring you a little joy. What color is accompanying you lately? What attracts your attention? Maybe you can buy pillows, candles, a vase in this color? Why don't you paint one wall this color? Maybe you have more money and can buy yourself a gift that you would like to receive from a man? The invention is yours. As an exercise of self-care, do something nice for yourself.

If you are a woman who buys something for herself every now and then, don't buy anything for yourself as a gift (but buy it for someone close), and what's there for you? Take yourself for a walk. Go somewhere you feel good, where you haven't been for a long time, go to the place you miss. Just be there with yourself. Maybe you want to go on a trip? Maybe, but go there alone!

I have an idea! How about taking a day off from work for yourself (as part of your vacation) and spending it completely in your own way, taking care of yourself? You can go to a coffee shop with you for a coffee and a cake, or you can go to the IKEA and wander around and look, or maybe you want to lie in bed and sleep in your pajamas all day in the middle of the week (i.e. on Wednesday)? Or maybe you want to sit on the sofa with a blanket wrapped around your legs and read a book all day? You're gone one day! You're gone! You've gone (to yourself)! And no one knows where YOU ARE, but you know that it is important that just be with yourself sometimes.[1]

---

[1] exercise 8

When you ask for help

Talk about yourself. Ask a loved one to talk to you and tell them how bad you feel. If you have never done this before, start. Be very specific about how you feel, what you feel, what you think. Tell the whole world about it. Speak right and left. Talk to women, men, loved ones, more distant ones, older then you, younger then you. It may turn out that they will bravely endure it and the world will not collapse at all. You can ask for support. Better yet, ask for a hug and accept it. This way you can feel embraced by the world. Wouldn't it be nice if the world hugged you and supported you? Get it for yourself. I'm sure there are people around you who would love to do that. Choose well though. Choose those who wish you well, who do not tell you what to do and what is good for you, who selflessly devote their time to you, who will gladly listen to you. Don't hang out with the overly smart. With those who know better than you, with those who feel better than you. Let there be those around you who just like you, do not know what to do, who want to accompany you in your decisions, whatever they may be. Let them be with you just like that, let them put their arm around you when you cry and let them not try to do anything with you. If they try, don't let them and tell them you just want their support.

Are you ashamed? That you're weak, that you're human? That you're not doing well? Or maybe you're just trying to cope like a human being? You're ashamed to be yourself, to be authentic, and you're not ashamed to pretend otherwise than everyone else thinks? Be ashamed and do it either way, and shame will pass quickly, because he is afraid of action.

Finally, ask for help. You are a human. Sometimes people need help, they make mistakes, they go astray, they need support. We are all, basically, small and imperfect. Only not everyone can admit it.[1]

---

[1] exercise 9

When you realize you hear voices

After you've already rested a bit, slowed down, talked about yourself, maybe you've allowed yourself to have difficult feelings, it's time to listen to yourself. Maybe you've already written a bit in your new notebook, maybe you can hear your inner voice better, which has been knocking at you for some time, and you've been ignoring it ...?

What is your voice telling you?

Mine says right now: *You ask a woman a lot of questions! Isn't it too much? Hmm... Maybe it's better that you ask a lot instead of talking a lot... Let her answer for herself... Let her look for wisdom in herself, not in you. After all, that's what you want her to listen to herself. And we made a deal, hi, hi, hi...*

And one day I wrote: I am close to the decision to separate from my husband. I want to go my way. I'm most afraid of hurting him. It gives me no peace. And deep down in my heart I want to be alone, I dream of my own apartment, order in it, silence and an armchair to read. I dream of being calm and joyful. After all these difficult emotions and dramatic moments - I dream of rest, soothing my heart, peace of mind and conscience. Yes, that's what I want. (...) I think what I need most now is to sort myself out and like myself, to learn myself, to create myself anew. I want to leave, not to hurt, but to build.

Today the youngest cried before going to sleep and said: Nobody loves me as I would like. I asked what it would be like and he replied: I don't know how to say it. He cried and fell asleep peacefully. I feel like him: no one loves me as much as I would like.

Today I am on my own. No one can tell me what I should do and in fact no one tells me directly - thank you dears for that! I feel strangely confident and calm. I'm walking through this situation alone, I don't know where I got the strength from and how I know what to do. I only listen to myself. I feel like I should follow this path, not deviate from it, even though it's damn hard. I get terrible feelings. I don't know what awaits me. But I won't know anything until I try.

These were my inner voices – I followed them, listened, did what they told me, took a risk. A little over a week later I wrote: *I made a deal about an apartment for rent, I'm picking up the keys in two days. It took me 3 days to find an apartment! Once I made up my mind, it just popped up almost immediately. The handle has fallen, it's done, I'll do it, I'm leaving, it's decided!*

The next evening my headache intensifies, it increases rapidly, I start to cry, I feel terrible fear, soon after I vomit several times, my head explodes, I cry, I feel small and lonely, on my own. I have chills and nausea, I'm shaking all over. I fall asleep only in the morning broken sleep. Tomorrow I'm going to look at the apartment, my new house. (...)

First night here. I didn't feel any change, no pain, no loneliness... I've been feeling lonely for a long time. Peace, quiet, I am preparing the apartment, cleaning, I feel good here, I bought a radio and a kettle - it's Friday evening, I'm listening to the Third Program Chart and I'm drinking tea. I'm at home. I fall asleep peacefully.

My dear, I'm not saying my path is the best, I don't know what yours is. However, I know that your inner voice will tell you. You can try to listen to it. All in all, you might not lose much just by trying. You can always withdraw, apologize, return to the previous state.

In addition to inner voices, I hear outer voices coming from the world. They are signs. Magic hints, coincidences, incredible situations, hidden magic.[1]

---

[1] exercise 10

When you discover life is sooo magical

Life is amazing. It doesn't go as we think it would. It surprises us with the course of events. Its meaning is hidden somewhere. A friend of mine just left my house and unexpectedly arranged a spontaneous full moon date with her own husband, from whom she has been separated for over 2 years. Today is the full moon. I believe in the moon. And you? I believe it exists, that it reflects the light of the sun, though they say it shines. During the full moon, I feel differently, sometimes more intensely. During the full moon, I work better, have more creative ideas and energy. I also have strange or terrible dreams. I feel different. Today is a full moon in Leo, whatever that means - supposedly important. They say it's a big time for Leo.

And I am zodiac Leo. It's hard for me to say how much I believe in zodiac signs, but I do believe strongly in signs. For me, all the signs indicate that by listening to myself, I create myself anew, and that's good. I feel good that my ideas turn out to be good when they're entirely mine.

I woke up with the dream in mind. I missed this friend's date. I called her and told her the dream and she said I was some kind of witch, that it was exactly like my dream. wow! I am a witch? There is something about it. I have a good feeling, sometimes intuition, sometimes prediction. I once told another friend of mine who was pregnant that she was going to give birth tomorrow. And she said: What are you! I'm due in a week, not yet... And the next morning she texted me that her waters had broken and she was going to the hospital with her husband. I knew that there was a full moon and that women give birth more willingly during this time. I once spoke to a midwife who told me that the delivery room is crowded during the full moon. So do you believe in the moon? It was such a combination of facts: her, the full moon, the short term to be resolved, and my strangely sure and calm feeling. Is that magic? Perhaps magic is the combination of all these things in the brain, but maybe somewhere else?

But I do know that a lot of what is happening is happening somewhere else (not in the obvious reality) and magically somehow. What is happening in my life right now is also like that. A lot of pain, difficult decisions, acting in accordance with (something that was constantly drowned out) a voice from within. And the result is stunning. I am where I am and I am writing to you. Although I would never have dared to write openly about myself specially not as much as I do now. Now I'm writing to the world of women. I share myself and I feel that it may be useful to someone. I don't even think what to do next. I'm writing and I don't know where it will lead me. I follow the voice from within and without. Behind the voices and signs I hear and see. Everything fits into a larger whole. My difficult story and my damn suffering and confusion start to make sense. If I had to experience this just to help you, then I am grateful to fate for such a gift. It's okay that he sent it to me.

Today I am. Now, I feel that it's good, I'm not rushing anywhere, I'm not waiting for anything. And my friends ask what's going on, they say that I have an amazing twinkle in my eyes, that I look beautiful. They ask if I met anyone. And I think - yes, I have met and I am getting to know and I am falling in love. Hi hi hi... I recognize myself![1]

---

[1] exercise 11 and 12

When you have men-(o)-pause

Hi hi hi… I have a men–(o)–pause, I've put men on hold. I live alone. The children are partly with me, partly with my husband. I gave up my previous life, took time off, abdicated, moved out, took a leave of absence. I took it brazenly, because I couldn't do it otherwise, I took it, and I didn't ask anyone about it, I didn't ask for it. If you want such a holiday for yourself, maybe do it better than me, ask, explain, suggest. I didn't have the courage, I couldn't, I didn't know what I wanted and what was going on. Now I know. And I know it's too late, that I hurt my husband badly. I have great remorse and regret for this and sadness when I look at him.

Not for a moment did I feel that it was a stupid idea. I didn't hesitate for a moment and I didn't regret it for a moment. I've been at home for a few months now and I live my own way. I create my own temporary place and I feel at home in this rented apartment, more than at home, in a real, beautiful home.

I have no one. And I don't feel lonely. It is what it is and it's fine. From the first day of being here, I felt a peace that grew in me day by day. Today there is much more. And the reward of this crazy decision is a greater sense of life, openness to what happens to me, joy, love, being a better mother and something that I can't name yet, something great. As if I was on a foreign trip and was just at my destination, in my dream place. I love to travel, but right now I am traveling at home, inside. What views, what grounds! I haven't been here yet, it's just weird and exotic here.

I don't need a man now, I have everything I need inside me. Maybe it's time for this men-o-pause. I've always been with someone. I've had a man by my side for over 25 years. I created myself as the one with the man. Maybe I was creating myself through a man? Now I'm alone and I'm grateful for that. What a state! Just me!

I really want and need it. I need myself and be with myself. Maybe you don't need it, maybe you have a nice relationship and you can enjoy it and you can thank your partner for being in your life. And in exchange for a men-o-pause, you can take, for example, a work-pause or a child-pause.

When you realize men are like cookies

For mental pain some people use different stuff to feel the relief; alcohol, drugs, shopping, food. These temporary things can help distract and calm your nerves. However, they act as something good only for a moment, then they start to do the opposite - they destroy you. I do not recommend these ways even for a moment. Although I myself used sweets to drown out my pain. I love chocolate with nuts and peanuts in chocolate, I also have a weakness for cookies (now I mainly use peanuts).

For a woman after a breakup, men can act as cookies. I also do not recommend. I don't think it's a good idea to have one relationship quickly followed by another. One man after another can super help in patching up the black hole. However, would a healthy man want to be such a patch? Is it fair to him, is it fair at all? Is a woman supposed to patch up her emptiness or rather explore it, recognize it, heal it? I think this is where the important work for a woman begins. A difficult, painful way of entering yourself, your pain, fear, feeling of rejection, feeling of being small, unnecessary, unattractive or bad.

And it's not the cookies that nourish the body. The cookies are just delicious. Fruits and vegetables are actually nutritious for the body. Cookies have no vitamins. Instead, they have a lot of worthless and harmful sugar. Eat healthy and wise, that's also about men.

When people ask when will you have your life together

Is making woman's life better equal to getting a man??? She may not even necessarily be happy, but with a man she must be. There is so much pressure. You are not of value in itself. You are valuable and truly feminine when you have a man. And we don't get into which one, and we don't get into whether it suits you. There is a man and there is peace. Your parents may be happy that you've made a life for yourself. For other women, you are not a threat that you will take away their husband. A woman alone who is happy is probably some madwoman or something, or maybe an old maid, or a young maid, or a homosexual, or a nymphomaniac. My therapist at the first meeting asked me if I was single! What a question for a married woman with three children and a marital crisis at that. Now I think I know what she meant. Yes I am single! And I always have been, even when married. This does not mean that I want to be alone forever, that I have decided to avoid men. I have a men-o-pause. I am here and now, I am alone, but not lonely. I have myself and we get along well.

There's an ad for a mental health drug on the radio recently. The dialogue between the ladies goes something like this:

-Mark left me.

-After all you've done for him? Take this drug and you'll feel better.

Meeting after some time:

-Annie, how beautiful you look! The medicine helped?

-Yes, thank you. And by the way, meet Filip.

-I knew everything was going to be fine.

So what? Only then will it work out well, when Annie will have a boyfriend? A total disaster. And men-o-pause? She didn't have any time to herself, she didn't breathe, she wasn't with herself. She immediately got into another relationship and that serves her well. Yyh ... And this text that she did so much for him! What did she do? She gave him children, cared for him, fed him, drove him to work, renounced herself? And Annie looks beautiful because she has a new man. She can't look beautiful without a man. I'm not talking about a drug for the psyche that makes you look beautiful and conjures up a new guy. Who allowed it to be published?

And here are my recent notes: November 11 - *101st anniversary of independence in Poland. Today I am celebrating Independence Day. I'm alone, but I don't feel lonely. I live alone and I feel the presence of many good people in my life. Someone keeps texting or calling: How are you feeling? How do you do? I'm smiling. Today is the second full moon in this apartment. And I am getting fuller. Tea from a friend with honey and lemon tastes amazing today.*

My life is in order - damn it! I don't have to arrange it again.[1]

---

[1] exercises: 13, 14, 15

When you realize life passes right now

My middle child wipes the floor with loud music. The youngest was dancing a moment ago, now he is sitting on the floor and arranging Lego blocks. I write in my room, it's so relaxed. Oh, I just had a fight with my middle child, but he's nervous, and so am I. Hmm... I was supposed to write about nice moments here and now, what a coincidence. The pleasant moment turned into a difficult one. Are we taking life for serious? Well, that's how it is. And so it is now. Now it's not always nice. The reality suggests something more. You want to write about the beautiful here and now, but there are also unbeautiful and difficult moments. You have to accept that as well. There are hard times, there are ups and downs, there are ups and downs. Yesterday I discovered that someone tapped my car in the back side and broke the light. It must have been somewhere in the parking lot. Someone did it and fled the scene. Coward, pig, goop? I'll have to fix it, pay for it, and I'll have to do it myself. First I felt weak, then sad, and then I gave up. This is something I had no control over. You have to accept it and move on. I also have to pay because I don't have insurance. Medium sings to himself, I think he got over it a bit. He entered the room and says something carefree. How nice that it's letting go so quickly. Time passes and difficulties with it...

A month after moving out, I wrote: *The dishwasher washes the dishes. Children play on the floor with a sleeping bag in throwing away garbage. Sometimes they pretends to be a garbage bag. They laugh out loud. I'm between a bath and reading a book. I write by the lamp. Water pours into the tub for a common bath for the boys with a green tea-scented sparkling ball. Candles are lit on the dresser. The oldest, a student, will arrive soon. Will be staying here tonight. We'll all play Monopoly Junior.*[1]

---

[1] *exercise 16*

When ideals is not enough

You were such a perfect couple – they said. Perfect? Have you ever seen a perfect person? And two? Have you ever seen a perfect relationship made up of two imperfect people?

Difficult ballast to carry - ideals. They collapsed with us and the world does not want information that we have failed, that something has gone wrong, that we have broken something good. The world also doesn't want that information that two cool people can go their separate ways, they can separate and live separately. The world wants them to always be together, to be proof of constancy, security and unbreakable love. People think of these situations as failures. I think it can be a chance for development and for a new life. Maybe separately or even together, but differently than before. After all, everything changes, there is no constancy, nothing is eternal. Change is not necessarily a bad thing, but change in a relationship between two people always brings drama, failure, and pain to mind.

And you might think that this is not the end, but the continuation of our story.

When you realize you might have never been here

My mom said: *Dear, I know what's good for you. I wish you happiness and I know what your happiness is - Well, Mom, I don't know if you know. Since I don't know myself. Mom, you fought for me like a lioness when you were three months pregnant, when the doctors wanted to remove me from this world without your consent. You knew what to do then. You said, you shouted, "I absolutely disagree!" It's possible that you instilled in me this struggle for survival. Thank you for this gift, for this moment, for your power and strength. You gave birth to a girl who became a woman. Just such a woman. You taught me to fight for myself, for my survival. Are you surprised that I go my way and that I live my way? Thank you for who I am and for where I am. You are a wonderful woman. My first woman ever. My shell, skin, ocean of love. I feel how much you love me and it is such a beautiful feeling that it is difficult to express it. Thank you, dear Mom!*

You might not be here either. You too are in this world for a while just like me. Maybe it's strange that you exist at all, maybe various circumstances did not favor you, but you are still there. Think about what to do with this gift, with your own life. You have this life to yourself, you can do what you want with it. You can enjoy it, you can complain about it, you can live the way others want you to live, but you can also live your way. And I'm sure the choice is yours. It's like a board game, you roll the dice and go. You don't know how many you'll roll or where you'll go, but you have the option to hate the game or enjoy it. You can wonder where your pawn is going, take chances, take risks, enjoy the road, be curious about what happens to you. Someday it will be over. And that's for sure, but now it's today and choose: you have fun and play or pretend you don't care and get tired inside every day.

Listen, do you know that you're going to die soon? We do not know when, but we do know that it will happen soon, because life on Earth is very short and passes quickly. How old are you? I'm 44 and those years have passed in the blink of an eye. I was little, then young, and now I'm more and more mature. For me, it's a good time to think about what and how to do next. A good time to set the rhythm of my life, the style of my functioning, priorities. I don't want to rush and waste time (mostly) to earn money anymore. I want some time for myself, I want to be closer with people close to me, I want to enjoy life now while I'm still alive. I prefer to read a book, play board games with my child, and dance. I have nothing to run after anymore. I caught up with the time. Is here. I don't have to rush, I can slow down. And what would you like?[1]

---

[1] exercises: 17, 18

When you think that you are stupid

If you think that there is something wrong with you, it always has the negative impact on your self- being. Think differently - your thoughts affect you. If you think that others are doing better, that they don't go through crises, that everything is somehow easy for them - then you are wrong. Of course, there are people who do better, and there are people who do worse. There's no point in comparing yourself to others. You look at other women and think: younger, more beautiful, slimmer... and what? And what do you get out of it? How do you see yourself?

One woman told me that she often said to herself, *"Oh, you stupid bitch!"* Apparently, her grandmother used to call herself that. Awesome! This is how she described herself when something went wrong, when she forgot something, when she accidentally broke something or when she made a mistake or didn't know something. Universal term, right? First of all, it's not nice of her to think that a cunt is stupid. Secondly, it's fucking sad. I have heard many other very strong and sad expressions of women towards themselves, which do not bring anything good, do not make sense and are often completely illogical.

Write honestly, in your beautiful notebook, what you really think about yourself in your heart. Write how you define yourself. First, focus on harsh words, sad thoughts about yourself. Be super honest, no one will read this (I hope). Then read aloud what you've written, tear out the page, and burn the words. Symbolically say goodbye to such treatment of yourself. Go to the garden or to the sink in the kitchen and, burning a piece of paper, apologize out loud to yourself for such cruel (or unkind) naming and treatment of yourself. Then sit down and write good and true things about yourself. Write what is cool about

you, why people like you. List 10 examples pertaining to:
- Things you do well (10 things you do well)
- What you have already accomplished (10 things you are proud of)
- What you think about yourself (10 new, nice things you can think about yourself)

After completing the task, make yourself a cup of tea, wrap yourself in a blanket and sit nice and warm for about 15 minutes in silence.

I thought I was stupid. Even when I did my master's degree twice, even when I became a psychotherapist, even when I passed my math exam with 5 (AP). I always thought I was stupid. It still happens to me, but rarely anymore. In general, I thought about women that they are stupid, that men have wisdom, and women are like their complement and are made for them. Nobody told me that, nobody taught me that. I just felt that way. That's the message I read from what I saw. Today I think I have wisdom, I do not consider myself wise, but I feel that I am not so stupid after all. And in my life I met many smart women and thanks to them I understood that there are smart women, and how!

And I started to appreciate this half of the world, such a beautiful half, but so beautiful inside. Women use hidden and different wisdom. It is not visible at first glance. They can combine experience, knowledge, senses in a slightly different way and from this they create a whole. They have amazing intuition, intuition, emotional tact. I think so. And are you smart?

I am reminded of the adorable fish Dory from Finding Nemo, who suffered from short-term memory loss. Was she stupid? She had memory problems, yes, but she had intuition and something else amazing: she only focused on the now. Because of this, she was fully herself, for her nothing else existed, there was no past, there was no future, she was spontaneous and focused on the current task. She wasn't afraid of taking risks, wasn't afraid of living, wasn't afraid at all. And her amazing lyrics: You know what you do when life is down? It's hard to say and move on. And her song: A fish likes to swim as long as it's alive. Sometimes the wisdom of life is somewhere other than in the head. :-)

And Winnie the Pooh - a silly bear? He's so simple that he's charmingly smart. *What day is today* - asked Pooh, *today* - answered Piglet, to which Pooh - *is my favorite day.*[1]

Don't be silly, we all know you are smart.[2]

---

[1] Winnie The Pooh
[2] exercise 19 and 20

When you give yourself a new name

My first name, given by my sister is Eve. When she was 8 years old she couldn't say the whole name (Ewelina). It stayed that way for the family, then for close friends, then the name went spontaneously into the world and the earthly family called me that, not a family of blood and genes, but a family of beautiful people I met on my way. Some are closer than family. Some brothers closer than their own brother. I am Eve to you too. From my surname, some people call me Sikorka (Polish titmouse). I love that term. This is my artistic pseudonym as a creative photographer Sikorka - Photo Flow (on Facebook), Sikorka Flow (channel on YouTube). And my quiet other name that I gave myself while writing this book, actually today, is Perseid. It's from the meteor shower (shooting star phenomenon) that takes place every year on my birthday, August 12th. It's a gift from heaven I get every year.

The description of this rain fits my situation on earth and the task I have undertaken in writing to you. And do you have a task? You sure do, you just don't know what it is yet.

As Wójcicki from the Copernicus Science Center said: *what seems to be a shooting star (yes, it has recently deteriorated) is in fact only a speck of dust (I feel so tiny too), often no bigger than a grain of sand. It falls into the earth's atmosphere (I fell) and due to friction with it, it heats up (creatively), it burns up (my aging and dying), and the trace of such a process is observed in the sky as a short, quick flash (maybe this, this book will be the following). I just checked the moon phase calendar and it turns out I was born on a full moon. But eggs! So here I am - fully female - Eve, Perseid, Tit.*

Perseida fits to the little girl that is still inside me. Ach! Dear, you have a name! Do you like it?

And what's your name? Maybe you like yours? Or maybe not so much? Find your new, different name. Give them to yourself. If you want. Maybe it's already smoldering silently in you? Maybe it will reveal itself soon? Do you have the courage to ask your friends to call you differently? Try to introduce yourself differently, sign differently. Of course, if you feel like it.

Please remember that everything I am suggesting here is an indirect proposition for you, a metaphor in itself. Search for your true self in your own way, do my tasks in your own way, go your own way. If I become your inspiration, it will be an honor for me. Copy it your way, be inspired as much as you can and create yourself new one in your own way.[1]

---

[1] exercise 21

When you realize you have a little girl

Little girl lives inside of me. She is gentle yet very smart. She is spontaneous, likes to have fun, loves to laugh and joke. She likes to eat ice cream and blueberries. She is a few years old, but can already talk. She says what she thinks. She gets angry, she cries, she is afraid. She's real. She doesn't pretend, she doesn't wear masks. Her name is Perseid. I come over to talk to her sometimes. We like our meetings very much. She lives in a small house that she built herself out of a table, chairs, pillows and blankets. She is such a little Niunia (that's what my mother called me) who sometimes needs my support, my strength and hugs. And I need her simple life wisdom. She is deadly straightforward. She has the gift of seeing complex things in a clear way. She can solve puzzles, go through mazes and connect dots, and she docs it in no time. Sometimes when she says something, the shoes fall off. She is hard to ignore, but it takes great courage to listen to what she says and act on her ideas. She wants, she knows she can, she hopes, she loves life and people. And she sees an opportunity in everything. In failures she sees learning, in bad people he sees good, in the past good moments, in the future dreams. Oh, I'm not afraid to dream. She's always dreaming and playing around. She likes to play princess. In this game, she has the power to get what she wants. Has the power to acquire new skills. She has the power to realize her own thoughts and dreams. She is beautiful, wanted and loved.

And your girl? What is she? describe her? Discover her, see what she does. Listen to what he says. Talk to her. Ask what she needs. Ask her a question. Listen to what she tells you.[1]

---

[1] exercise 22, 23

When you discover the roots of your power

Ask someone close to you to slowly reads the following text, and let yourself fly to the land of imagination and look for your place of power. Create a nice quiet atmosphere. And take a journey inside yourself. You can record your voice on a voice recorder (you have it in your phone) and then listen and follow your voice in your imagination.

Close your eyes. Imagine you are going on a trip to a beautiful place. Sit back and let your imagination run wild. Imagine your journey. You're going there alone. What means of transport and where will you go? You're on your way. Watch what you see, experience the journey. This is a journey to a beautiful place, a journey for you. You drive or you walk... and you arrive home. Slowly come closer. See what's around him. Maybe there is a beautiful garden, see what grows there, look around the house. Then go inside and explore it. Look at the rooms, windows, furniture, walls. Once you've explored all the rooms, enter the kitchen. There's a woman there. He invites you to tea. Sit down and be with her. You can ask her a question. Listen to what he tells you. talk. After the conversation, say thank you and slowly return to your here and now. Come back to reality, breathe and open your eyes.

What did you see? Write it all down in your notebook. Describe your conversation, your feelings, your discoveries. It is possible that you have symbolically met yourself in your inner home. The woman may not be like you, but she probably represents your inner wisdom. And home is your inner home. This is your place of power, you can come back to it in your imagination whenever you want to rest, you can also travel to it and to yourself, in difficult moments in life, to ask something important. There is your wisdom and there it is safe. This place is yours and no one can take it away from you.[1]

---

[1] exercise 24

When you read 34 books and that's still not enough

You know, when I was going through hard time I was reading a lot. In about half a year, I read 34 books! I didn't have time for that before. Nothing has changed since then, and yet somehow there was time to read. This letter is a mix of what I have read with what I have experienced, with what is going on with me now and with what I do in my work as a psychotherapist. During the therapy of others, I don't talk about my life, but I allowed myself to do it here. What the hell. I felt such a need, I felt that my story could be important to you, not just my wisdom as a therapist. It's a bit against the flow, against everything, and a bit against myself. I did not expect such a turn of events. However, when I started to face great difficulties in myself, and then found a way to overcome them, I felt that maybe this is the way to you, that you will hear me in this way. By the way, you're listening to my story, thank you for that. Even if you don't understand or feel me, at least I'm writing to myself. Everything is sorting in my head now and forming a larger whole… At the end of this long letter, I wrote for you the titles of the books I read. There will be a little more than 34 of them. Because my crisis lasted longer than this six-month mega book passion. I've read before and I'm still reading - but at a more normal pace. I recommend them all as required reading. Hi hi hi… I didn't even know that there are so many valuable books. Lots of important things and people I discovered on the Internet, some of which I also listed at the end of this book. Everything got mixed up in my head. Sometimes I don't know what I read where, where I know something, where I heard something. From this mixture, this letter to you was created. From this mixture, the whole me was created. I apologize to the authors for shortcomings in quoting and pointing to sources in the right places. I'm very sorry. And to this you have to add people-books that I read thanks to the fact that they opened up to me. They are patients and friends and people from the network. And also conversations with loved ones and their huge support, which completed this list.

When you admit you are a sensitive person

Has anyone ever told you that you are oversensitive, overreactive, that you have problems with your emotions, that you feel too much? Have you ever thought that there was something wrong with you, that you were some other, some mismatched, incompatible with this world? Or maybe you sometimes thought that you are super special and no one understands you and others don't even see your uniqueness?

Check if you belong to the group of highly sensitive people. I have listed the readings for you at the end of the book.

I am tired of unwanted sounds - noise, bars, places with a lot of people, crowds. I don't like fuss, supermarkets, loud disco music, disco polo, I don't like jazz either, and hi hi... In addition, I hear sounds that others cannot hear, the ticking of the clock, sounds from outside the window. I have a keen sense of smell, eyes sensitive to colors and shapes. My body is also very sensitive and this fact causes me a lot of inconvenience. I don't like when the youngest kicks his legs when he falls asleep and accidentally rubs me with them, I don't like dancing with strange men who are too close to me, I don't like how they gently touch me when they pass through the door. I don't like touch when I'm stressed and stuff... I have to have comfortable clothes, my music in the car, silence and order at home (small number of items). Too much stuff distracts me and excites me. In order to focus on a task, I need to be comfortable around me. When I'm texting, I can't hear what someone is saying to me. When I'm listening to someone, I don't like having the radio on. When I play a difficult board game, I can only listen to music in English.

Polish words from the music mix with those from the game. Come on, just! As I write, the children are in another room, the door is closed, the radio is off. I get tired easily with sensory impressions, I'm easily overstimulated. When this happens, I quickly become tired and super irritable. I get scared easily, and that easily escalades. And I don't like it very much! I need a good night's sleep to function properly. I have many dreams. I think a lot and have a very vivid imagination. I do not like horror movies. For me, television and news from the world are horror, which I digest only in the radio version, without a picture. Strong images stay in my mind for a long time or forever, so I have to protect my brain from them. I used to think that I was very nervous, that I was weird and antisocial. Now I know that I have this genetic endowment - my grandmother had it, my dad has the same. Each in its own way, because this condition manifests itself individually. In my office, about 70% of patients have it. And the vast majority of women. This sensitivity applies to sensory stimuli, but also to thoughts and feelings, i.e. the world of the psyche, contacts with people and spirituality. Do you have something similar? And ... and pain, you can feel it more than others, physical pain and mental pain. Fortunately, I have a good tolerance for physical pain - phew. I can relax at the dentist. I bravely survived three natural births, and in all this confusion, the worst for me were catheters and blood sampling - i.e. foreign body interference in my body - needles, but I feel mental pain beautifully and perfectly.

If my description somehow fits you, then you are probably a highly sensitive person, not overly sensitive or overly sensitive. And you're not exaggerating, you just haven't learned how to function with your sensitivity in this world yet (despite your age and a lot of life experience, hi hi hi ...). You keep trying to fit in with the majority, and somehow you fail. You do not allow yourself to be different and you do not accept that you are constructed differently and have different needs. Read about it and think about it. I have already accepted and even liked a different me, different from the world. Different does not mean worse, just different, and at the same time, really unique.

It is possible that you are giving yourself a lifestyle that overwhelms you and may last for many years. For me, it was over 20 years of living in a rush and self-abuse. It is possible that many things are beyond your strength, but you endure them bravely. It is possible that this has led to a difficult moment in your life. Maybe you should do something about it and take a serious look at how you function on a daily basis. Such overload (and additionally misunderstanding yourself) affects other spheres of life and strongly disturbs relationships with others. It can lead to a breakdown, depression, professional burnout, loss of the meaning of life or the breakup of a relationship. Also, it's serious.

If it turns out that this is the crux of your problems - as long as you take good care of yourself - you are saved!

There are big pluses from this high sensitivity, e.g. great creativity, perceptiveness, quick learning of new skills, sensitivity to danger, predicting the future and the consequences of events, intuition, empathy, seeing nuances and non-obviousness, the ability to empathize with others and understanding without words, mind reading (I exaggerated a bit here), better insight into yourself, sensitivity to the needs of society, curiosity about the world and refined bravery and endurance, the ability to adapt to new conditions, openness to experience, developed abstract thinking, courage to cross borders, consent to life against the general trend, great individuality.

I am happy with this turn of events. Thanks to this sensitivity, I am who I am, I am where I am, I photograph, I work with people and I am writing this book and I dare to reveal myself because I see the sense in it. I am an example to you that you can live with it somehow. As you know, it wasn't always easy for me and I had to learn myself. And I learned the hardest and most valuable lessons very recently.[1]

---

[1] exercise 25

When you feel comfortable with silence

I love silence, I love being alone. I'm never bored. Even when I have nothing to do and rest, my mind is so curious that you can't get bored with it. In silence I rest from stimuli. I don't have a TV, I only listen to radio or my favorite music. I have plenty of it for every mood, every day, but silence is the best. This is my medicine for overstimulation, overload, fatigue. I like to lie on the floor in silence. I read books in silence.

Do an experiment and do not turn on anything in the house all day. Be silent and only with yourself. Take a break from stimuli. Allow your mind to travel deep within yourself. It may not be easy, especially if you have been jamming something in yourself for many years. You'll probably hear what you don't want to hear, but if there is, it's important. Look at this. Write about what appears in your silence. What's going on in your silence?

We live in a difficult world and in difficult times. All the previous years were also difficult. We are not suited to the world. They don't teach us in schools how to live, how to adapt, how to fit in, or how to rebel against something, or what it's worth rebelling against. Parents make sure that we finish school, college, get a profession and earn for ourselves. Ah! What an interesting perspective. Live to survive! The world is cruel, unjust, unpredictable, diverse and unclear. There are a lot of people in the world and everyone is different, but at the same time the expectations for everyone are the same. We are supposed to go to work 8 hours or more, sleep 8 hours or less. We're supposed to have houses, cars, cool furniture, cool appliances, and cool shoes. We're supposed to have children and earn a living. We have to earn money for society, taxes, insurance. We don't always get enough of it for our own lives. We are happy when we have enough to pay for food, rent and gas. And holidays are a rarity. Did someone teach you how to rest? Has anyone ever told you how precious silence and listening to your own mind are? Did anyone tell you what to do when you get lost? What do you do when you get tired of life?

Turn everything off, rest and wrap yourself with silence.[1]

---

[1] exercise 26

When you clean around then you clear your mind too

Dou have chaos around you, but you like to have everything in order? Tide up. Are you as annoyed by lying objects as I am? If your items do not have their place or there are too many of them, this is a good time to clean up. The order in objects, in the material world, in papers, in clothes, in your home affects your mind. Start by getting rid of the excess. Remove all items from your home that you don't use (and still think you'll need someday). You can start by putting them in cardboard boxes and taking them to the basement or garage. After a few years, you can safely throw them away (without looking inside), but you don't have to wait. Look around. Like what you see? Do you like your home? Would you like to change something in it, improve it, repaint it? Make a change in the material space and it will help to make further, deeper changes in you. The first step - unnecessary annoying items, dumbstands, dust traps. Take everything off the shelf, from the rack, throw it on the floor, look through it, throw away the mass and leave only what you really like. Attention, I let you throw away the gifts and sentimental things that remind you of old times. To hell with it! What old times? What are the old days for? Do the present tense at home.

I like it when I have low furniture, and objects in the furniture, and nothing on the furniture. Window sills empty or with a few candles. Clean floor. One desk lamp, small items in boxes. I don't have an ideal house, but I have the way I like it, I have it so that it doesn't piss me off. If some disorder doesn't bother me - it's fine, but if it annoys me, I clean it up so that it doesn't annoy me. You can work on the place where you are every day. Clutter is also a stimulus, clutter tires the mind. At least mine. And also a bathroom, more clothes in the closet ... A nice read on this subject is at the end of the letter to you, at the end of the book.[1]

---

[1] exercise 27

When you loose 11 lbs

ow is time to tide up your body. You want to loose 11 pounds? Almost every woman wants to lose weight. I wanted a lot. My body grew under stress, because under stress I was eager to eat sweets and unhealthy snacks. I was doing well, I was having a good time. and ass! And my ass grew, hi hi hi ... I couldn't lose even a bit, despite the movement that I made with this body. Until finally I came across a diet, or rather a fruit and vegetable fasting by Dr. Ewa Dąbrowska. And I took the challenge for 21 days. I will not write you here about the details, if you want, you will find information about it. You know where to look, but the diet is simple, wise and paradoxically nourishing for the body. 21 days of vegetables and water cleansed my body but also cleared my mind! This fast is cathartic and medicinal. During the fasting, the well-being and vitality increased day by day. Witchcraft? Ah, how it changed me! It's hard to describe. I have infected several people with this topic, who are also delighted with the effects. I can give you a guarantee, if you take it honestly, you will surely lose weight, feel better and cleanse your body. It wasn't very difficult for me, I'm almost always a vegetarian, so eating vegetables wasn't a big deal. It was hard to give up coffee (two days of headaches) and refocus my head on new ways of thinking about food. It is important then to leave the fast, which lasts as long as the fast itself. And then he will stick to healthy, new eating habits. I lost 11 lbs and the weight has been maintained for 2 months, because I care about what I eat. It's super cool to have less waist and baggy pants and a smile on your face because you managed something that seemed impossible. You too can lose weight. This diet will work! Just check if you can use it for your diseases, if you have any more serious ones, and determine how long the diet is recommended for you. The full length of healing fasting lasts 42 days. I chose 21 days because I had nothing to heal from, but I wanted to cleanse my body and lose a few extra pounds. They were completely unnecessary! A little thinner, you will be healthier and happier and proud of yourself. If you are anorexic, don't do it. If you are very slim, consult your doctor (*or pharmacist, because any diet, if used incorrectly, threatens your life or health*).

I guess I don't need to add how great I am? And my friends ask me how I managed to look so cool. Now I'm eating dried mangoes and cashew nuts while I'm writing, sipping tea with lemon, it's 7:22 pm and there will be no dinner. And my body thanks me. And I thank my body.[1]

---

[1] exercise 28

When you have so much to do, but you just put it off for later

Backlog is like a massive mess in the house. They clutter and tire the mind. Make a list of things that have been waiting to be done for years and slowly do what you have been putting off. Check off with a tick and enjoy the growing number of ticks! This is very satisfying and it brings a lot of fun. It even has a name. Not the ticks, but procrastination. This is something that produces stress, tension and strain. Like untidy items in the house, unfinished washing dishes, unglued baseboards, when several years have passed since the renovation.

All in all, it's a nice order waiting for you from every side. We have order at home, in the wardrobe, order in thinking, in feelings, in relationships, in food, in lifestyle. We are behind in reading, in taking care of ourselves. Sometimes we hear someone say to a depressed person: get over yourself. Now it occurred to me that you can take care of yourself seriously, that is, take care of yourself in many aspects. It's such a nice take on yourself - such a better treatment of yourself and catching up with many years of your topic. Maybe your toenails are waiting to be groomed, maybe you can take a nice bath by taking care of yourself? Arrears can also be your needs, your desires, your dreams. Maybe you've been thinking about something cool for a long time and you've been putting it off for 10 years. There is no then. Is now. You don't have to wait.

Besides, if you don't do the old stuff, there's no room for new stuff. If you don't finish what you've started, you won't have enough strength for the next one. When you finish something, you will be satisfied just like with this diet. You will enjoy it and feel relieved. Maybe you have some unfinished major life or professional tasks, some studies, some driving license, some renovation, some important conversation? Don't put it off. Act now. Take small steps and tick off. And then celebrate, reward yourself, and thank yourself.[1]

------

[1] exercise 29

When you dare to care about yourself and you start to believe that your own way is the best

We need a lot of courage to take care of ourselves in today's world. Sounds weird, right? But that's truth. People are afraid to show that they are important to themselves. It's easier to take care of someone else rather than yourself. It's easier to be nice to someone else rather than to yourself. It's easier to compliment someone than to say something nice to yourself in the mirror. It's unpopular to think positively about yourself, it's weird to even think positively at all. Complaining, whining, talking about what are you missing, reproaching yourself, insulting yourself – this is popular. Fortunately, going to a therapist and working on yourself is becoming more and more common. However, even with a therapist, it's a tough thread to work with: to find cool things about yourself.

Taking care of yourself means going against the flow of the river. Thinking only about yourself is selfish. At the beginning of my difficult decisions I had a huge sense of guilt and fear that something bad would happen to me. I was afraid that the world would punish me for my selfish behavior, but in return for this, every now and then I had nice surprises, nice coincidences and the kindness of the world. Everything fell into place like a puzzle, and small inconveniences quickly turned into a new quality of a different life. I'm still scared. I still feel like I'm hurting myself by taking care of myself. I still get stomachache whether I'm doing the right thing. Every day, however, with more and more peace, I find the meaning of what is happening.

I have dared to take care of myself and I am starting to believe that my own way is the best. I dared to listen to myself and go my own way. I guess it's logical that my own way is the best way for me. Isn't it? If I feel better and better, more and more at home, this is probably the best way to go. And the growing peace and serenity give me courage for next days.

One day I wrote these words: *Not finding any other solution to the stalemate that had been going on for several months, I moved out. Now I'm alone! How quiet here. How nice here. What a view from the window. The newly renovated apartment welcomed me warmly, gave me shelter, promised me peace. I am here alone (or with children). Six nights have passed. I calm down and, what's worse, I don't want to go back. I look out the window and look for a view to the future. I don't feel abandoned, neglected, regretful, no one leaves me here. I'm with you and I'm not leaving. I am reading.*

You have a choice, you are the choice.[1]

---

[1] exercise 30

When you give yourself life

*F*ew weeks earlier I dared to write: *In internal pains, in pains of the soul, heart and head, in unbearable and almost endless pains - I gave birth to myself. I gave birth to a little girl. She is beautiful, innocent, vulnerable. When she sleeps, she breathes lightly. She has smooth skin and gray eyes. She screams a lot when I leave her. I can't even go to the toilet without her. We're still together. I take care of her, wash her, feed her. I look deep into her sparkling eyes and say: you are important to me, you are not alone, we will stick together. I see peace in her eyes. Some ocean of calm, a deep ocean, until I shiver, until I'm a little afraid of this depth. What else will I see there, will I not drown in it? I'm sitting in a gray tracksuit, in a gray armchair, I have gray eyes and I'm writing. My gray life is looking for colors for me. The eyes are dry now. Good thing I have a little baby. I have to take care of her, maybe distract myself from the pain a bit, I'll take care of her. Little Niunia now sleeps sweetly and safely in her crib. She breathes lightly. I touch her head gently, she has such soft blonde hair. She needs me, she can't survive without me. I have an important job. Taking care of her. I wonder what she will be when she grows up?*[1]

---

[1] exercise 31

When she starts living with you

When you give this little girl life, describe it in your notebook and take it to a place of power. Again, ask someone nice to read the following text to you slowly. Or read it yourself, and then go into the world of your imagination and take care of this little one, giving her a home, shelter and a sense of security.

Sit comfortably and close your eyes. Imagine you are going on a journey. Repeat this journey from the previous visualization, take it slow and savor the time. Watch what happens to you. When you get home, look around, see if anything has changed. In your arms with your baby, explore your place of power, your inner home. Find a place for a little girl. Maybe it will be her room, maybe a nice little corner. Keep her warm. Put her to sleep. Let him sleep in peace and quiet. And now you take care of yourself, do what you want. Sit somewhere, go somewhere, do something. Look what's going on. Be yourself and enjoy the moment.

Once done, write down these images and your feelings in a notebook. I won't remind you of this anymore. About the notebook. If it has become your beloved life companion, then you know what and when to write in it. One wonderful woman once told me in a session that for her a notebook is like a colander - it drains the water and leaves the precious pasta. She took it nicely.

And you think about what was nice in your inner home, what details you remember and try to organize something similar in your current reality. Even symbolically.[1]

---

[1] exercise 32

When you finally decide to become a princess

Who did you want to become when you grow up when you were little? Do you even remember times when you were just a little girl? I wanted to be a princess hi hi hi ... Well, not only that. I also wanted to become a cleaner, because I really liked how the cleaning lady in kindergarten swept the floors. When she swept the garbage from under the tables, the effect of her work was immediately visible. It was very exciting for me. Then I wanted to be a teacher at school, in the younger classes, such a nice, wise and understanding lady, then I wanted to have a shop... and I had other ideas for myself...

And you? Who did you want to be in the past? What did you play when you were a teenager? What did you like to do? What impressed you? (I'm not writing you to write it down in your beautiful notebook anymore, because I don't think I have to...) Sometimes big girls implement girlish ideas and in their adult life, they play what they used to play in their childhood: shop, house, in school, in horses. This is often a great idea for life, for a profession or for a passion! What did you dream about as a girl? [1] You know, I have my own room with a lovely crystal lamp in it. A few weeks ago I bought myself a princess bed. The remorse kept me for over a week. I was wondering if I could afford it. Can I afford such a gift for myself, such a soft and pleasant rarity? Or should I sleep in an uncomfortable bed? For punishment. Does being a princess at my age (hi hi hi) fall out (where does it fall from, where does it fall into? - what a dumb term!)? I dealt with the remorse, the bed is standing, I still have something to eat, I sleep soundly in it and dream my stupidity in it. It's white, wide, and just for me. In the morning or at night, a little man quietly creeps up to me and gently pulls

---

[1] exercise 33

back the covers to cuddle up to me and mix his dreams with mine. And in the morning, the palace lamp shines brightly above us. I can afford to buy something that I can't afford... hi hi... What! Today a new quilt, pillows and new pillowcases with flowers arrive. Here I am, a princess without a prince, a princess in her crib, a princess in her life.

Princess archetype hi hi hi... There is no such thing, but we can create it here. Why not? Well, symbolically, the princess embodies power and possibilities, strength of character and self-confidence. A little princess doesn't have to be a beef ass. After all, she can be like Brave Merida (from a fairy tale), who, along with other candidates, claimed the right to apply for her own. A girl who plays princess wants to believe that she can do anything. He plays the game that he can do everything, that he gets what he wants from the world. The princess likes beauty, she surrounds herself with pretty objects, she likes order, she likes comfort, she likes nature, flowers and animals, she likes people, she is kind and has a good heart, but the most important thing is that the princess knows that she is the most important. And he's not ashamed of it. She is confident, likes herself and respects her decisions. He has his own decisions and is not afraid to use them! The princess thinks about others and puts her energy into doing something good for the world. She is not (only) selfish, the world, people and goodness, justice and peace are important to her.

And the princess is the girl from the moon.

Would you like to become a princess? Hi hi hi... I am here, with my decisions, with this palace lamp and with this beautiful bed... Yes - I am and I am a bit ashamed of it. I am afraid of the judgment of others. I am afraid of ridicule and criticism. I am afraid that someone will point out my selfishness and ruthlessness in pursuit of my own goals. I'm scared as hell, but it's too late.

And now a task for you. Think back to those years when you were little. Remember your toys and your dreams. What toy did you miss or dream about? What would you like then? Or maybe you didn't even know then, but now you know what a gift this little girl would love. Think about what she would like to get and buy her a gift. For real, not pretend. Buy a gift for a little girl. Go to the toy store and look for something nice for her. Or go online and find a handmade stuffed animal or doll shop. These are only hints. Do it your way and actually buy her something and then give it to her.

I see! And I? I haven't done this task yet, and I often ask other women. I will do it with the greatest pleasure.

I found a rag doll hand-sewn in Poland by a Polish woman - she's awesome. She has a pink dress with watches print (a symbol of beautiful age), a removable coat and a hat with a scarf and a handbag. wow! I'll order it. What a joy! My little Baby is jumping and dancing with joy.[1]

---

[1] exercise 34

When you are looking for a mom

Do you know you have a nice mom? Maybe your mom is like that, but I'm not thinking about that mom. I'm thinking about Mother Earth. You are her daughter, she brought you into this world and she loves you very much. She has tasks for you and wants you to develop, to help her create this world. Due to the fact that this is a mom who does not use human language, she speaks to you in a different way. It gives you signs, signals, speaks to you through your experiences, thoughts, feelings, through time, seasons, elements or dreams. You are not easily accessible. The signal is constantly interrupted by gray reality.

Did you know that you have a cool and smart grandma? And again, I am not thinking about your earthly grandmother, but about Grandma Cosmos. Grandma Cosmos is the mother of your Mother Earth. They have a good relationship with each other. Grandma loves mom and all her other children. And he has an incredible weakness for grandchildren. How is it grandma. Grandma has it even harder, because to hear her you have to completely abandon earthly frustrations and jump to another level.

Try contacting your mother first. Are you ready? Please write her a letter. Tell her what's going on with you. Describe how you got lost in your life and why. Write about your dreams and anything else you want. Write from the heart and don't think too much. You can ask her questions, ask for support and stuff... The rest is up to you. Good luck.[1] After 24 hours, sit down and write a response from her. Listen to the silence and write what you hear. Go a bit crazy - because I'm offering you something crazy. Normally people don't write to Mother Earth, they don't even write to their birth mother, so go crazy. I'm very

---

[1] exercise 35

curious what you'll reply.[1]

And in order to meet Grandma Cosmos, I suggest a lonely walk in the bosom of nature. You can talk to grandma through trees, wind, sand, stones. Silence is the guide here, there are no words. You can go for a walk at night to watch grandma in the sky. And listen to what he tells you. Attention! He can say difficult things, because Grandma Cosmos is not a stick. Take your courage and go for a walk. I hope this won't be your only walk like this, just your first. Ah, how I wonder what he will tell you! And you?[2]

If anyone is interested, I am a believer - I believe in Mother Earth, Grandma Cosmos, I believe in the power of the Moon and dreams. I believe in fairy tales, in the human imagination, in ancient myths, in goddesses and witches. I believe in people. And I don't have to believe in God because I know he exists. I am sure of his existence!!! I do believe that God is good and that he is love. I believe that it is for all people and that there are ways to it, including non-religious ones. I feel His presence and love very strongly! I understand the teachings and attitude of Jesus better and better.

---

[1] exercise 36
[2] exercise 37

When the universe has your back

Universe has my back. It has yours as well, because honestly why not? It can be, and probably will be, that going your own way will open up new territory for you. And then the kindness of the Father of the Universe will be activated. I have experienced this many times on myself and seen it on other women. When women chose, took risks, acted their way, took care of themselves - miracles began to happen.

And I wish that for you. You know what I mean? I think of those magical coincidences when you meet someone you just need, you hear something on the radio, a phone rings, the book you've been waiting for and for which you're ready and open now falls into your hands. After my session in One Brain therapy, which concerned the desire to change my job, I left the office and got a phone call with a job offer. It was something amazing! I still work there today! My breath stopped for a long moment from the great sensation. Or now,... I can see a big girl singing with a little girl on the Internet right now: I will overcome the storm, when you are next to me, you complement me. I am crying with emotion, because I feel that they are singing about the topic that I am just describing - a good relationship with each other. About the bar between the big woman and her little inner girl. I feel the strength in this and I feel that you too will overcome the storm when you acknowledge the presence of this small part of you. It doesn't matter that the author of the song could have meant something else. I am experiencing it now, my emotion, my tears and my feeling that the universe favors me and gives me signs that I am doing the right thing by following my own path. And by the way – the lady is so beautifully moved, as if she met her little self - it's so nice to look at!

Today I wrote a few words: *I am very at home and strongly myself. I am calm and excited. I am writing a book for women, for myself. I feel that what I do is important. I'm almost 50 pages now. I don't know how it happens, but I know exactly what to write and in what order - it feels like it's writing itself. I started on the first day of my period, with first blood on February 2, 2020, right after the mega new moon in Aquarius, before the full moon in Leo. I write every day. When I'm not doing it, ideas come up and I write them down right away and it all meshes beautifully with reality, arranges and composes into a whole. I feel part of something bigger. It was as if something was guiding me by the hand and telling me what to do. I can hear and see clearly all the directions, I can hear the inner voice and the outer voices. I feel an important part of the Great Universe. I feel that the universe favors me, that I have a nice connection with it in myself. I like Him - this Universe and I feel that He likes me too. I was given a task and I fulfill it with joy. I feel like I will be writing throughout my menstrual cycle. I wonder if it will? Are there enough ideas just for now? So far we are on day 10 and everything is going according to plan - not my plan. I don't plan anything here, I surrender to the whirl of events. I give up and feel like a winner. It is interesting. Thank you Universe. Daddy Universe? Your little molecule.*

Time has turned and it is now. I used to write about my past, now I write about my present. Maybe we'll go on together? Yes I think so. It's very exciting. I'll keep you posted on what's going on with me. Tonight is the first night in the new, fragrant princess bedding.

I woke up later than usual... The bedding was excellent, but the dream was terrible. I dreamed that a friend of my patient's husband wanted to hurt me sexually. I was running away. I must have run away because I woke up. I recognize that I have escaped. I felt as if one man had sent another after me. And my patient's husband has just been led out of the house by her. The husband may be dissatisfied with her cooperation with me, that's the way it is sometimes.[1]

---

[1] exercise 38

When someone says this is a stupid idea

A Changing woman can enter a lot of discomfort to her husband's / partner's life. Accustomed to a certain state of affairs, your man (if you have one) may be amazed at your new ideas. Another close person (for example, your mother) may feel anxious as you begin to grow and change. You're telling someone something they don't want to hear. You reach for your needs, which he is not used to, you make some other, strange new movements, you disturb comfort, you disturb peace and sense of security.

Men sometimes don't like the changes their partners make in therapy. I don't know what to tell you here. Will your man accept you the new one or will he be able to handle it? I don't know, the risk is high. Honestly, you can lose a lot, but you can also gain a lot. The choice is yours anyway and depends on you. You have a choice, you are the choice. And even if someone close to you tells you it's a stupid idea, you can go your own way and keep your own side. Because for you, it might be a smart idea.

Now for the man's job. Look at your woman as an independent being who can and can live without you. She is different than you and you can love those differences. You can't have her to yourself. It cannot be your property. There is no certainty for you. Once you may have said: I take you for my wife, but how can you take someone? You didn't take her. She moved in with you, agreed to live together. She didn't give herself to you. And if she gave, it's bad, because she shouldn't, because she can only have herself for herself. What do men need now? Now they do not hunt, but work and bring money. The woman also brings money. What role do men have for women now? Sense of security? Is it? What can you give her that she can't get herself? Who can you be to her? You can love and show love. You can be an accompanying and supportive presence. Yes, you can be a presence. You can be a walking love and kindness. What does she need that the world won't give her? What can only get from you? What do you need from her? Who can she be to you? Think and tell her exactly what you need from her, from her and why from her. Modern times are new, what can modern women give? They used to give the warmth of a home, now they go to work. And the home hearth is your common plot. This world has been new for some time. The old roles are not working, and the new ones have yet to be defined. Talk to each other about it. Sit by the fireplace or by the radiator or on the sofa and talk about yourself, about your needs, about your roles and whether your life suits you. If so, enjoy it and celebrate - because you have something special! If not, look for solutions together. Be in this together, listen to each other and respect each other.

When you ask questions and the world doesn't give an answer

Today in my office I had a meeting with a new woman. And then one of the last meetings with a woman who ends a two-year process of finding her way to herself. Ah, what a confluence of energy it was. The energies of this circumstance converged. One said she wanted to grow up and stop being a little girl, the other said she was calm, stable and confident. The first cried out of sadness and grief. The second was moved by her achievements and laughed out loud, hearing what she said about herself at the beginning. And me in the middle. Thank you women for your trust and such openness! It is a great gift for me to be able to participate in your maturation. Be an adult for you. And again, I read it as another sign from the world that is saying something to me. You can clearly hear what he's saying to me. Right?

And you can now ask the world a question and listen to what it answers. Formulate them specifically and say them out loud. And then register the different signs and put them together in your head. Look, listen, dream, speak, feel, write, read, act, create. Good luck. And I'm curious again about the answer the world has for you. your discoveries. It can be a long road, this your way of finding yourself. Give yourself time. In therapy, it usually takes about 2 years. Without therapy, it can be much longer.

I once saw such a huge poster in a store with the words Go your way and I had shivers down my spine and I stood at it like a dead man. At first I felt a great agitation within myself, only then did I understand that it was a sign for me.

And today I picked up some signs that I should talk to you about sex. It was my dream and conversations in the office. I will save this important topic for tomorrow. Now I'm going to go to bed and hope I don't dream anything. Or will some signs come again? Lately, almost all the signs I meet on the road are about what I should write to you. Thanks to this, I have absolutely no problems with the vein. It is everywhere, surrounding me, cornering me and following me as I flee. I am a participant in a larger task and I am sitting in the center of events. Like when I was pregnant and I didn't know what was going on, and I felt part of a greater miracle, and I couldn't get over that I was part of it, that everything was happening as if through me, without my participation. I go to sleep and every now and then I get up to write down the thoughts that come to me. Is it some kind of witchcraft or what? An open notebook, always at hand. I think that somewhere for you there is also such a magical place. I think that you too can feel a small part of a great whole and find your sense of being here. He will certainly be different than mine and you will reach him differently than I - that is, in your own way. I wish you this with all my heart![1]

-----

[1] exercise 39

When you feel like talking about sex

Do you feel like talking about sex? Probably not. What's more: about your sex? Oh! What a topic. You are a sexual being whether you like it or not. You have this beautiful nature in you, you have the gift of experiencing the spiritual with your body. You can feel closeness to another person through your body. You can invite someone over and let them make themselves comfortable. Such an experience can be a relief for you, release tension, a sense of incredible security, fun, joy, closeness and love. If what I'm writing now doesn't really apply to you and you experience the sexual sphere differently (not beautifully), then it's disturbing.

Maybe your sex is fulfilling a marital duty? Maybe you're doing it because you're afraid he'll go to someone else if you don't give him one? Maybe your sex is associated with fear, is forced, you don't like it and you don't like how your partner treats you? Maybe you're doing it for him, out of love, and you'll work out a bit and he'll be happy? It's all bullshit! There are no such marital obligations!!!! You don't have to give him anything, because sex is not giving, it's meeting two people. Sex cannot be out of fear and for someone. Your body doesn't like it very much. And if he's going to go to someone else, let him go! Oh mother, how terrible it is what I write, how terrible what I hear from women!!!!! I am telling you very simply and clearly now. Don't do it, and that's the only thing I strictly forbid you to do! Do the rest your way, it's your life, but I don't agree that you agree to unwanted sex. It's just wrong and doesn't make sense! Sex is as natural as eating, pissing or pooping. It's pointless to force it. It's like someone wants you to eat candy if you don't want to and you've had enough of it and it's too sweet for you. It's like someone telling you: go pee now, I'm sure you want to, and if you don't, then do it for me. Sex is a natural human need that can be satisfied and the other person and their willingness to do so are useful. It's a beautiful sphere and you don't have to and shouldn't. This is a beautiful sphere of your life, enjoy it and have fun with it. Sex is like dancing. Maybe someone invites you to a dance or you invite someone. You go out on the dance floor when you feel like it and dance with your whole being because you want to. You are yourself in dance and you are spontaneous. It's not good when someone says: Dance spontaneously, dance with me - now! And you agree to it. NO. Simply do not.

Good sex is a beautiful and spontaneous approach of two people who want it. The result of this rapprochement is the meeting of two bodies in love and peace. Or have you experienced the opposite in your life? Or many times? Maybe someone used to hurt you a lot (dad, brother, uncle), or maybe someone still hurts you? Maybe you agree to painful suffering because you have no other idea? Because you don't know there's another way? If so, be sure to work on this topic with an expert in the head. Absolutely - you can't do it yourself. Until you do, don't read this book any further. Until you stop violence in this area (even the invisible one), don't read on. Because the rest of the letter is for you Unharmed. You will not progress further in your development if you allow yourself to be hurt further. And if you have any minor problems (doubts) in this area, think that there is something important that you would like to change, talk to your partner about it. Sit down and talk calmly, very directly and looking him in the eye. Say what you need, what is important to you, what you would like to change, what you miss. Reveal intimacy needs, expectations, reveal sensitive issues. Speak straight, don't imply. If you feel that you may be addicted to sex and getting into sick relationships, seek a specialist in this field and stop the speeding destructive train.[1]

---

[1] exercise 40

When you set boundaries

Do it in all phases in your life. Are there things you agree to do but really don't feel like doing them? Are you doing something that hurts you, annoys you, tires you, destroys you? List 7 things you agreed to in your life but didn't want to. Describe the consequences of this for you. Now write down 5 things that you will definitely not agree to in your life. You can be proud of yourself for not agreeing to these things anymore. Congratulate yourself. Now, write down all the things you are okay with in this life and would like to change. Start small and don't ignore them. Small steps will teach you to take big ones and give you strength. Record all your successes in this area. And enjoy them by celebrating your own way.

Today I was with the youngest at the doctor's and I remembered my stick trauma. Do you have it too? When I was little, the doctor would put a stick in my mouth to check if I had a sore throat. She was in too deep. It was so unpleasant that I did not want to go to the doctor and said: only without the stick! My dear, wise mother taught me to show my throat beautifully without a stick. I practiced it bravely until I perfected it. My kids can do it too. Mouth wide, tongue out and you say Aaaa... while inhaling air at the same time. Simple? You can? And I've never allowed myself to put a stick in my mouth, Dr. I'm proud of myself. This is my important limit. Maybe even my first important line that I didn't let anyone cross. Then I asked my close men (and sons) not to tickle me, not to scare me, not to touch me suddenly, not to make fun of me. This is my important territory, my body, my head. I want others to respect my boundaries. And you, where are your limits, small ones too? Do you respect them? Do you think you're overreacting and letting it go? Don't let go dear, respect yourself and your physical and mental territory.

When you finally stop being just a good girl

Once in kindergarten at the speech therapist my son misbehaved, he smashed some pieces of paper. The lady complained. When I asked why, he replied: *with my speech therapist, I had politeness in the weak part of my head, mom.*

Girls, in our culture, are not taught to set boundaries. Girls are taught to be polite, kind and helpful. And preferably still strong, brave, durable and smiling. Like a stamped foot, they hear: the anger of beauty hurts, when they say no!, they hear: give in, let go, you are wiser. When they want something for themselves, they hear: it's selfish. Little girls are supposed to be good. And the big ones, already trained in this, know that it is necessary and socially desirable. Big, they know that they should be polite, that they have to do something and something falls out or not. I hate all these expressions: I have to, it's appropriate, polite. First of all, polite - it means that she does not get angry and does not set boundaries. Secondly, it is appropriate - that is, it is supposed to do as someone expects it to do. It's not right to think like that!!! It's harmful! And it still has to - and to hell with all this! Nothing has to, really! Do you still want to be good? Because I don't. I can be kind, kind, helpful and loving. But not polite. There is a book with a good title: *Good girls go to heaven, bad girls go where they want.* Beautiful, right? And it speaks for itself. Good girls have no limits. They don't defend themselves. They are not themselves - they are for others. They are silent - they don't say what they think. They smile when they should actually be crying. They don't cry because it's not appropriate. They don't dance - because they should be serious. They do not get angry - because the anger of beauty is harmful. Good girls get mixed up; they don't know what's right for them and what's not. Good girls care about what people say or think. Good girls are frustrated and have a lot of regrets. Good girls don't ask for help because they can handle themselves and are brave. Good girls feel like they don't really exist. They feel unimportant and of little value. Good girls are very sad inside. So I suggest that you sometimes have your politeness (somewhere!) in the weak part of your head![1]

---

[1] exercise 41

When you are in the best age of your life

Do you realize you are in the best age of your life? In the most suitable for you. That's why you're having a crisis, because you don't know it. Well, you're having a wonderful time. You live in this world, you have a body, a mind, you feel and you are. This is a good time for you to be here. And for you, your troubles are a gift, you can thank for them. Well, maybe you'll do it a bit later, because now it's probably hard for you to see that what happens to you is a gift. Have you ever had difficult situations in your life? Have some difficult experiences taught you a lot about life? Or maybe only difficult experiences were really important teachers for you? Wait and see what all this is for.

If you're the same age as me and you're around 44 (10 less or more, it's not a big difference) then you've probably come a long way. It is possible that you have big children, or they will be big in a moment. I have a little different, because I have a large, medium and small. It is possible that you have a profession and have experienced many (life) disappointments. You probably already know what you don't want. You may not know exactly what you want, but you know a lot about what you don't.   And that's something. You've tried a little in life, you've eaten a little bread. You can't be young and with a lot of life experience. You can't turn the river with a stick. You go forward, like Dory the fish: It's hard to say and you keep swimming. You are here, at your age, at a beautiful age, the best age for you. You may not agree with it, but these are facts. The facts are not disputed. Think about what you can influence and what you can't, and focus on the former. Be glad you're alive, because there are many who are no longer here and were younger than you.

So? Your children are grown-ups (if you have them), already brought-up (or almost), you know what you want, now it's time for you. Are you ready for it? You always dreamed about it, and now it turns out that you may not take advantage of it. You are in the right place and time for you.[1]

---

[1] exercise 42

When you are changing, just as women do

The world is changing. *Women are changing creatures.* And that's good. You want to change a lot, if you weren't fickle, you couldn't do it. So it's nice that you're changeable. Enjoy it. They say that the only thing certain in life is change. Maybe someone will say: but you changed, you have lost your mind hi hi ... Okay, let them talk. And you have the right to change. I once heard something cool: *actually, there's no need to worry about what people say, people are different, so they will talk differently.*

I like changes. I used to say so often, but not anymore, because the last changes were so difficult that I don't think I liked them. Change is life itself. Do you like life? Life is changeable! The weather changes, the seasons change, time speeds up or slows down, thoughts, feelings, people change. As my beloved friend Ewa wisely said: *In fact, you can't predict anything in life.*

A woman is emotionally volatile, she has constantly different moods, right? Women have new ideas. They are often the ones who drag their men into the field: new. Often, fortunately, men are grateful to them for it. A woman is variable in the monthly cycle. Within a month, she transforms several times and becomes as if different many times. And here I send a great expression of sympathy towards the partners and respect for their patience. How do you stand it? I don't get it very much. There is not much constancy in a woman who still changes throughout her life. In different periods of life, it takes different forms of its personality. She was different as a girl, different as a teenager, different as a young woman. And also, maturing to femininity, it can also become a different person. And that's what I want to tell you. This stage in a woman's life, when she is about forty, is probably the most difficult time for her, right after adolescence. It's a replay of puberty, because it's something very similar: Saigon, madness, chaos, doubt, getting lost and looking for yourself. The Crisis of the Beautiful Age is rather not beautiful. It is difficult, but maybe, out of this chaos, something beautiful will emerge.

It is possible that you do not know yourself a bit, your needs change, priorities change, the pace of life changes. You may be reluctant to accept these changes, but again, these are facts. There's no point in arguing with them. Certain things happen in the world, and in you too, whether you like it or not. Perhaps you want and need change. It is possible that you want to quit your job, take on a challenge, change your profession, develop a new passion, change your place of residence. You may be wondering who you want to spend the rest of your life with. It's possible that you don't even know what you want yet, but you feel like you need a change or you'll go crazy. I understand you pretty well here.[1]

---

[1] exercise 43

When you are celebrating love

My poem for Valentine's day:

I came to you in the summer, cheerful and naked...
I left crying, wrapped in my coat, on a cold winter morning...
I left all the seasons in your place.
Now I'm back home...
Although I've never been here...

I love American Holidays! Today is Valentine's day. Some men say they don't like this holiday because it's American. They don't like Women's Day because it's communist. Why not celebrate love? The best thing that ever happened to us? I like that day there. Well, maybe not this red-heart decor, but I like love and celebrating it. Love is nice though. People meet to refresh the fact that they love each other, that they have a priceless gift. They sanctify the feeling that arose between them and nurture the fire of this miracle. It's just beautiful to me. And by the way, I will share with you my view on other American holidays. Halloween - the celebration of death. A reminder about an important topic that concerns us and which we would like not to think about. Through play, children get used to such an important topic. There is an excuse to talk and the psychological ground is prepared. For me, it hits the spot. And then Thanksgiving - that's the shit! People meet each other to thank each other. Mommy, how beautiful. It is a pity that we did not accept it. We Poles are not yet ready for such a holiday, we are not ready to thank and be grateful. What a pity!

So if you feel love, celebrate it, preferably every day, remember it and cherish it. Because I already know that love can be neglected, lost, love can be destroyed. You can't feel love even if it's close. So if you feel that this is your holiday - I congratulate you and I envy you.

When you marry yourself

What would happen if you marry yourself? What kind of spouse would you be to yourself? You can safely treat yourself as a life partner. You can't run away from yourself, you have to live with yourself somehow. You can get married, in other words, make a vow to yourself:

And I swear to you love, fidelity and honesty... and that I will not leave you until death do us apart.

You can promise yourself the latter, but can you promise it to someone? What else would you like to vow to yourself, what would you promise yourself? Be a tender lover for yourself, take care of yourself, love yourself as someone close to you.

I decided that throughout the period of writing the letter to you, I will buy myself fresh flowers. There were two tulips already, and today I have white roses. There is always something beautiful on the dresser with candles and pleases the eye and heart. I feel like I was with myself during my engagement period. I get to know myself, I listen to myself willingly, I still want to be with myself, I take care of myself, I buy myself gifts, I am my girlfriend. I'm thinking of getting myself an engagement ring. Yes, laugh, I laugh too, hi, hi, ...

Awakening love for yourself will probably be a long process, especially if you didn't have much of it as a child.[1]

---

[1] exercise 44

When you get yourself from the net

The world of the modern network of interpersonal connections is fantastic, that's the world of quick information and many possibilities. We've got a tool that can take us anywhere. We can move around the world, we can see everything, we can hear the music we want, we can learn new things, develop passions, meet people, earn money. We may have a sense of power and a problem to feel human again. We can get very lost in this network of connections. I know many people who have their world and their head more in the computer and phone than in the real world. And yes, they know a lot... but they live as if they weren't there. They disappear during a conversation or right after a family dinner. They relax, check something, buy something, read something important. Only... Only... They are not here and often they don't even know it, they don't feel it, because they are at home. I also fly away sometimes. Because the other world is not television where you watch something that is on. There you watch what you want, what you turn on, but only theoretically, because the network draws you in and offers new options. And you go there, just for a moment, and you stray from your own track and the original theme, because theoretically you want to. And then it turns out that 4 hours have passed. And your head is a bit dizzy and you're slightly tired and you haven't done anything, but you're tired and you won't do anything else today. How about another movie while you're here? You may feel that you are in contact with the world, that you talk to people, see them, but you will never get real, human support there (unless it's a therapy session via Skype). You will never feel real contact - like in real life. You'll get part of it, but only part of it. You can feed on particles. You know, in this multi-dimensional world full of possibilities, you can feel very lonely and different. You can get lost in this world. And I suggest you take yourself out of the net, go for a walk, invite friends, eat breakfast with someone. I suggest that you significantly limit your time on Facebook, YouTube (or other such places) and searching for something on the Internet. You can even count how much actual time you spend there versus here. And watch what your children do. Play a board game with them. When was the last time you went for a regular walk? When did you create something together?

And I just ran out of Internet on my phone and immediately, somehow I got more time. For you I have an exercise - experiment: Take a week (or at least one day) break from the media (TV, Internet and Internet on your phone), you can leave the radio and music, but not much. Enjoy silence and reading. See what happens. How much time will you have, how much energy, what ideas will appear for yourself, what will you do with yourself? Are you up for the challenge? Such a challenge - you outside the network.

And then you can think about changing your lifestyle. If you waste yourself and your time on unreal nonsense, fictitious contacts, unnecessary information, silting up your mind - change the way you function permanently and be careful in this matter. Do not go to bed with the phone, turn it off completely at night, put it on a shelf at home. You can also throw away the TV or move the computer to another room. Do something about it if you're overreacting. Your mind will thank you for it. When you make a clear change, you may experience improved attention span, memory, and logical thinking. You can also feel the flow of time that you have been missing and do something really valuable with it.[1]

---

[1] exercise 45

When you start doing well with your emotions

What does it mean to do well with emotions? The psychotherapist is talking to you hi hi hi ... Well ... The world of feelings is very rich and colorful. We have a lot of feelings and they have a lot of shades. They can have different intensity and sometimes they are completely unlike each other, even those with similar names. Sadness, unequal to sadness. Feelings are. they just are. And they actually do. They come and go. Often they come to tell us something, to give us a clue to action, sometimes to protect us. Feelings speak to us, and we try to drown them out because we think it's wrong to feel. We think that the way we feel, there is something wrong with us. Not so? We learned this in childhood, when our parents ignored our world of feelings, when they suppressed this sphere in us and when they told us that you feel bad, or that you feel bad. As adults, we have a hard time admitting how we feel. And a human, not a robot, after all!

And dealing with feelings means accepting them and reading them correctly. And here a good therapist will come in handy, because, unfortunately, the topic is muddy and you can fall deep into the past, right up to childhood. Dealing with feelings is not about controlling them, but paradoxically, consenting to feelings and experiencing them (sometimes without control). Such true consent results in greater self-knowledge and greater self-power.

Today I felt very sad because something went wrong, and I really wanted something and I cried normally on my princess bed. will you believe? Me, the great therapist hi hi hi ... And then I wiped my tears and made myself tea with lemon. And I know what my feelings told me. Among other things, that not everything in the world can be my way, and it will not be. Stupid world! A 44-year-old woman who cries because of this! Embarrassing! Now I feel at peace, where has the sadness gone? sailed away? *You know what you do when life is down? It's hard to say and move on.*[1]

I believe that accepting the world of feelings in oneself and honestly admitting to these feelings, especially the difficult ones, is the direction of self-love. That's right, about this wedding with yourself. Can you vow to support yourself in difficult times, not to blame yourself for it?

And I also think that we women, not robots, are like nature in the emotional sphere. I think a woman is like a volcano. Sometimes dormant, sometimes active. Inside, there is a lot of buzzing and eruptions occur from time to time. These eruptions are natural, not necessarily desirable. Does anyone ask a volcano why it's erupting? It explodes already. People generally don't like volcanic eruptions. However, this does not mean that they are not part of nature. During the explosion, the woman throws out accumulated feelings and tensions with great force. And after the explosion, for a while, she is calm and discharged.

A volcano woman can feel like a madwoman in the world. He often feels that he exaggerates, that he makes scenes, phases, nativity scenes. He may also hear such words from others. Unfortunately, in this madness there is no acceptance for her feelings and states and it is harder for her to draw wisdom from these situations. Because if she herself believes that something is wrong with her, she works to stop exaggerating, and does not penetrate into what is actually happening to her and what her own feelings communicate to her. And feelings speak. Feelings are signals. For example, they say that she doesn't want something very much, they say she is treated badly, they say which way she could go to develop herself. Feelings also tell about the past that some unresolved issues and problems demand their turn. Sometimes they are indeed too intense for today, but that's because they resemble some unhealed wound from the past. This is where psychotherapy comes in very handy.

I suggest you try to read what your emotions are telling you. The ones that are repeated and the more intense ones are especially important. Don't ignore yourself, don't pretend to yourself that nothing is happening if you feel intensely. If you feel, it's important to you and you're not crazy because you feel. You are a person, a woman, a person, someone who expresses himself and communicates with the

---

[1] A quote from movie pt. *Where is Nemo,* dir. Andrew Stanton and Lee Unkrich.

world through feeling. Take care of this sphere, explore this part of yourself. It's part of your life! Piece of you![1]

---

[1] exercise 46

When someone sticks you with the knife

The transparent trauma. There's a kind of trauma from childhood and life that you can't see. They are small difficult situations, barely noticeable, that prick like pins, repeat and sting in exactly the same place. You can have several of these places. And although you may not have had a lot of painful, great, difficult experiences and traumas, you may have had invisible traumas. They are in a way more difficult to treat, easier to overlook, ignore or belittle.

An example would be when someone close or not, in childhood (or even in adolescence or adulthood), laughs at you from time to time. Maybe it's not too hard to feel isolated feelings of humiliation, being ridiculous, inadequate or not fitting in. Being ridiculed, however, is a very unpleasant experience, which in the very situation can provoke a smile and at the same time build tension and stress. You can get lost in it yourself and ignore the seriousness of the situation. If this situation, in which we experience a short-term but deep prick of a thin knife, is repeated, a deep wound is created. Painful with each subsequent prick and even with a light touch. These knives pricks create an invisible trauma. It is not known why the woman then cries when someone says something funny about her. It is unknown why she feels a lot of tension when she hears someone laughing next to her (often she thinks it's her). It is not known why he reacts strongly to not very strong words, or inadequately interprets someone's words and believes in these interpretations. And yet, she may not remember who did this to her. Maybe the older brother, who was also a child, stuck a knife in it and doesn't remember anything about it anymore? Maybe it was a few people at school or kindergarten? Maybe it was the first boy who said that he loved you very much and wrote beautiful poems about love, and at the same time he was sticking little knives innocently because he wanted it to be fun?

If sometimes something upsets you and you don't understand why - it can be an invisible, knife trauma. If you have a few of these sore spots in you and they're telling you because they're left untreated, it's important to identify and heal them. A sensible head specialist will do it with you. He can't do it himself. There must be another person with it. He'd find the wound, clean it up a bit, apply some comfort ointment, and then a plaster of understanding. And it will heal nicely. And then, you yourself, you will tenderly exchange a slice for a fresh one a few times and you will be as good as new.[1]

---

[1] exercise 47

When you write a script to your own life

It's your job, this script. Nobody will write it for you. And if he writes, it may turn out to be kitsch. What movie do you want to star in? What movie is your life? How do you write a script for yourself? Come up with a title for your movie and tell a bit of the plot. Is it melodrama, horror or comedy? Or maybe now there will finally be a twist after a boring beginning?

Who are you by the way? Can you answer this question? Not really? I can't either! I do not know who I am! I know my name, where I was born, where I live, how many children I have, what my shoe size is. I know how old I am, what I like and where Iceland is, but I don't really know who I am. And it doesn't bother me much. This question is too difficult for me. Maybe I'm too stupid for them - and that doesn't scare me either. May I not know something? What I do know is that I am and I know a little about what I am.

And I am looking for an answer to the question: what am I for? That's actually what I'm most interested in. What am I here for? What the hell is my job? What's the point of my being here? Perhaps this letter will partly answer that question. Maybe I'm here for you. You are for me too, you know? Thank you for letting me write to you. Thank you for being. You've come this far reading my words... Thank you for reading me. It is thanks to you that I discover my meaning. I hope that you, thanks to me, will be closer to you. Are we made for each other? We women should probably be closer together, don't you think? In this world there is so much unhealthy competition, comparison, evaluation, criticism, dishonesty, disrespect. Did you know that women can be cruel to each other? have you experienced this? That's why I thank you for being you, because I know that somehow you are similar to me. Since you have endured so many of my words, it means that somehow I don't annoy you very much and somehow you understand what

I write. If this is the case, then it is a phenomenon, because we support each other. I you and you me. I feel good energy from you. I know you are your grandmother. It's nice that you are here and it's nice that you have yourself, don't waste it. You are unique and unrepeatable, one of a kind. Keep it up. Don't change and be who you are. Because you have a kind of perfection in you. How do I know that? I don't know, but that's how I feel.

To search for an answer to the question: why am I here? I used the Gallup[1] defines my five strongest qualities. There I found important tips for myself. I read the results and thought: how do they know so much about me? And then: why didn't I know this before?

Because we have a task to discover - our life is a task. The message of this task is hidden deep in our hearts. It's like a maze again. The answer is not usually obvious, but the tasks are very different and complex - just like yourself. The tasks are individually tailored to different people and are unique (!).

Can you read the message encoded in John Lennon's life? Can you read the message encoded in the life and works of Johann Sebastian Bach, Witkacy or Rembrandt? Some messages are harder to decipher and everyone can understand them a little differently. However, you can live your life and not read/decipher your own message. Pity. It's a waste of life, for a life without a task. It's like a meaningless life. Unless someone lives with meaning, that is, meaningfully, but does not know it, and is sad that he does not know what he lives for. So the

---

[1] *The Gallup Test is a common name for the psychometric instrument CliftonStrengths, formerly called StrengthsFinder, developed by the Gallup Institute, which forms the bulk of its revenue. The test was invented by Don Clifton and is known also as the Gallup Strengths Assessment or Clifton Strengths Test. It is an online personality-assessment tool that focuses on 34 themes that make up the user's personality; Gallup uses the tool as part of its consulting. The results of the test are intended to help individuals understand their unique strengths and how they can use them to achieve their goals and improve their performance. The test is widely used when assessing candidates or considering employees for internal promotions. The article available online, for the day 25.01.2023* https://www.gallup.com/cliftonstrengths/en/home.aspx.

answer to the question: why am I here? - seems to be very important.

And coming back to the movies, I know (feel) that you write the script of your life and you play the main role in this film. Good luck at the premiere. May you enjoy watching it.

When you realize you don't even know who you are

I received an answer to my question today: Who am I? Answer inspired by a late-night 4-hour conversation with a friend-brother from Norway. Well, I'm nobody special. Perhaps I would call it more that I am Something. For as I delve deeper into my mind, I find that it is deep and boundless. My mind is not quite me. In fact, I am a temporary dwelling for some greater consciousness. I am the temporal flow of a higher being in this earthly world. So you can say that I am nobody and everything. I am also you, in part, we have a connection in our mind and I feel you even though I don't see you or don't know you. Now I am a medium for the flow of information to the world of women. I am not the author of this information, I just mixed it up and spat it out (no offense). I am a mixture of what happened to me, whom I met, a mixture of different thoughts and events. The content flows through me, it's not mine, but it's nice that it came to me. Now it flies to you with all its power. Maybe you would like to be such a flow too? Like this, just different. Because everyone has different tasks for themselves.

Are you a nobody too? Do you also sometimes experience amazing, greater sensations than yourself? Do you have a connection with the universe? Where is it located? In the heart of? Or maybe in the eyes? Look at yourself in the mirror today, longer. Feel yourself, say something to yourself, be with yourself, don't take your eyes off, don't be afraid - it's only you and you. Approach the mirror and experience the depth of your eyes up close. See what you'll see there. Feel what you feel there.

So when someone asks you who you are, you can confidently and proudly say that you are nobody (and in the silence of your heart know that you are everything).[1]

---

[1] exercise 48

When you hear: oh, you and your friends

Is it something your partner would say? Don't let him! Unless they are really not friends, but "fellows" - throw them away from your life. They won't come in handy.

Women can give amazing support. I have been gifted with many amazing women who (I don't know how they do it) make me feel that I am okay the way I am. They are neutral and don't tell me what to do or what I should do. They don't talk much, they just are. They ask and are interested, they listen. After meeting them, I feel energized, I feel I have given something and taken something. And that's what I call friendship. My lovely women! If it is you who is reading, you who were my support at my home, for coffee in the city, on a walk in the mountains or on the phone - thank you for being here. You are a great gift to me. It is also thanks to you that I write my words. It's because of you that I dare to be brave. Be closer to you every day, my dear!

If you, after meeting a friend, feel pumped up, abused and misunderstood - then this is just a friend. Throw her into space! It will not be useful in life, and it will even hurt.

And if you have friends (maybe even forgotten somewhere) then refresh these acquaintances, take care of them, cherish them, invite them and enjoy them. And ask: What's up with you? How are you? And if you don't have it, look for it. There are women in the world similar to you - with a heart in hand, with cordiality in the pocket and with openness in the head.

And I have three male friends. It's just a departure. A man who, like a friend, understands what I'm talking about. Great experience! And on top of that, she keeps boundaries and doesn't expect my body from me, doesn't flirt and makes me feel all right. So true friends can be female and male - they are all great!

When you are simply not sure

When you are not sure if you want to buy the dress you are trying on in the store - don't buy it. When you're not sure if you want to take the new job that's been offered to you, don't take it. When you are not sure if your husband is a good candidate - don't marry him. When you're not sure if you want to go to that party, meet that man, wear that blouse, don't. Don't do what you're not sure about. Because if you are not sure - it means that you are not sure, or rather you do not want to. Principle: I'm not sure, it often works in life. Do what you are sure of, the rest is a waste of your time. And you know you have less and less of it. You no longer have to tense up and do something for someone all the time (unless you want it with all your heart and you are sure of it).

You may think that the decision you have in front of you will bring you closer to something important in your life. Manage your time and spend it on really valuable things. Choices are usually hard. When choosing something, you can ask yourself: do you want it, or maybe others expect it from you, or maybe some advertisement made you dizzy? Or could you live without it?

Write down these questions for yourself: *Now, if you died, would you feel that your life was fulfilled, that you filled this time on Earth with something that you are satisfied with? If you could live again, would you make any different decisions? Answer these questions and look for answers to this: how could you truly feel fulfilled?*

And in your life, when making decisions, you can follow this signpost: *Does what I choose direct me to my fulfillment?* [1]

---

[1] exercise 49

When you discover your passion

I did so many different things in this field, I had so many different passions. Sometimes I feel ashamed that I wasted my time, that I was constantly grabbing for something new: photographing, drawing, swimming, creating various trinkets, wreaths, sewing. After some time, I always changed my passion for another, and abandoned the previous one completely. I finally made a circle. I went back to photography, which I had a little fun with the Zenit camera when I was 16-17 years old, and then I used other equipment. And it turned out that I have another passion right next to me. It turned out that I don't have to search anymore, because my passion is women and working with them. I didn't call it that, but these topics have always fascinated me. Recently, in fact, I noticed that what I do makes me very happy. I found that I no longer need to search for anything. And the combination of photography with women that I still have in mind for now gives a good kick. So I already have. I was there, but I didn't see it. But I'm glad! And keep looking if you haven't found it yet. It's not true that I wasted my time. That's all it took for me to grow up and get to what I have now. Without passion, life seems weak to me: work, home, children, husband, shopping, eating, sleeping, work, sometimes holidays. It's not enough for me. I want more from life. My life wants more from me. You can have a passion or earn money from your passion. Both options are fine as long as they suit you. Passion is something that turns you on, occupies you, draws you in, develops you, makes you happy and gives you meaning. Passion makes you feel alive, that you lose track of time, that you fly away, that you express yourself and give something of yourself to the world, or the world gives something to you. And if only someone forbids you to have your own exciting world - don't let it. Maybe you've already tried different things, maybe you already have something, maybe you're dreaming of something. Try, search, act, don't give up. For you, life without passion can be very, very difficult. As for me. Neglecting yourself in this matter can cost you a lot, because in passion there are often hidden answers to important questions. There may be a trace of an encrypted road to yourself.[1]

---

[1] exercise 50

When you feel something good coming

If you follow my suggestions and implement my ideas, then you are already in the process of change. Do you already feel that something good is happening, that it has begun? It is possible that your thinking has entered a different track. Or is it the hardest for you right now? Because knowing yourself hurts a lot sometimes. If this reading does not bring you much and you are a bit tired of repetitive threads, my style of writing, thinking, or the atmosphere, then take it easy and put it on the shelf, or give it to someone who may be more useful. However, if you like the tasks and you do not find time for them, then put the book aside for a while, catch up with the content with your actions and come back to this moment when you are ready. And if you're walking with me, slowly and carefully, you've come a long way. You have your beautiful notebook and you do not hesitate to use it. In fact, it's already heavily engraved. Maybe you're in therapy and working through some difficult issues from your past. Maybe you already have your new name, you met your new Mom and Grandma. Maybe you enjoy contact with Father Universe and hear what he is saying to you. It is possible that you have already bought yourself a few nice little things and already have a gift for your little one. You already have a place of power that you sometimes go to, and sometimes you meet this little girl in yourself and you do something together. You agree that sometimes it is difficult for you and you see some greater sense in it all. Sometimes you feel like a freak - but somehow you feel happier and livelier. If you're here right now, that's fantastic. Congratulations and I love you very much. It is a great joy for me to be your travel companion. This is my 15th day writing to you. We're halfway there. I still have a few topics and tasks for you, but I know that I will improve the previous entries in the meantime, because more important things appear in my head. So you have less than half left to read.

If you don't have your notebook yet - this is a good time to put the book down and go to the store. This will be your diary - you will write down things that are really important to you and thanks to it you will remember them better.

When you start liking your body

Your body – a very important and hard topic. Or maybe I am wrong? Many women have a big problem with the fact that their body changes over time. Our culture prefers young and pretty women – we know that. Your efforts for the body will do little. You can, of course, take care of your skin, hair and figure. Of course you do, do it. Just don't get too fixated on it. After all, you can't change the course of events (the course of aging). You can also focus more on something you can influence. You can invest in intellect, language learning, memory exercises, acquiring knowledge or new skills. The mind is like a muscle, unused - it disappears hi hi hi ... Seriously, it is known that exercise gives a lot. You can learn at your age too. Possibly a little slower, but it's also possible that you'll be able to make a healthy selection of what's worth remembering and what's not. And then it can be faster and more productive.

Do you like your body? No? Why? Do you like? Phew... that's great. Your body is a very useful carrier of you around this world. You probably have two arms and two legs. You have a head, a brain and a heart, thanks to which you think and feel. Thanks to that you are. You also have eyes that see this world and its values, you have ears that sometimes hear amazing sounds. You have a mouth with a tongue inside, which is used for various things, e.g. to recognize flavors, to grind food delicacies. You have such various efficient offal that are used for digestion, regulating hormones, enable you to live. What more could you want? You wish you had nice hair, bigger eyes, longer legs. Well, nature has not bestowed? And what did she bestow?

List all the parts of your body you like about yourself. Maybe the neck, maybe the toenails, the shape of the ears, the belly button... Then write a letter to your body thanking you for being fit, for being alive in it. Also tell him what you think about him so heartily that you get angry with him, that he is not prettier, that you regret that he is getting old and stuff ... Write what you want, talk to him, with your body. Finally, write your conclusion or keynote, and if it's soothing and wise, stick to it. You can write this thought down on a piece of paper and stick it near the mirror in the bathroom. You will see her next to you when you look in the mirror. Guests will have fun.

And I don't like aging either. Who came up with it? Or maybe someone smart who wanted to tell us something? Anyone who sees sense in this? Or maybe it's such a message and a challenge for us, and if you pass this maturity threshold, you will still be rewarded? It is possible that there is greater peace and consent to each other and to inevitable changes. Imagine yourself completely at peace with this process. Imagine that you don't really care what you look like, but you care about how you act. Imagine yourself wrinkled, old and cheerful, full of love and light in your eyes, in the company of people who love you.

Find a picture of an older woman like you would like to be in many years. It's about looks combined with serenity or something else that's important to you. Print this photo or organize it and hang it on the wall, or put it on your desk (or maybe hang it in the bathroom). And then talk to her in your mind about your dilemmas related to your body.

And I offer you one more task - take a calm, mindful bath. Create an atmosphere in the bathroom. Dim the lights and light the candles (minimum 5 candles). Ask household members not to disturb you for at least 59 minutes. Leave your phone and books in your room and go there alone. To the temple of water and earthly corporeality. Add some fragrant salt or other nice aromatic to the bath. Stay warm for a long time. You are in the water, like in the mother's womb, the water soothes and envelops. Wash slowly and carefully. Spread the soap on yourself gently. Seriously, do it very, very slowly and carefully. Look at the parts of your body, send them nice thoughts, thank them, massage them, cherish them kindly. Relax to the max without rushing anywhere. It's you and your body and you're fine.

And now a few words about the face. Your face accepts wrinkles - these are features of events that have happened to you in life. The feelings you experienced. The face is the page on which your life is written. They say you can tell a lot from the face. I agree with it. Now, when these features are produced more intensively, it is especially important what you experience, how you think and what you are like. Now everything writes faster and clearer. So if you want a nice wrinkled face, make sure you laugh a lot, relax a lot, live a lot smarter, and create your life your way. Then the joy of life, serenity, life wisdom and personal freedom will be written on your face. Does it make sense to you? I know that it depends a bit on you how you will look as an older person, what your face will look like. Your face and look depend more on it than on a good cream.[1]

______

[1] exercise 51

When you practice Hygge

People in Denmark practice Hygge. They have one word that inc-ludes several terms: comfort, bliss, relaxation, unhurried joy, comfort and coziness. It's all in one word. This is the whole philosophy of life and the art of spending free time in happiness, family warmth and closeness with a sense of physical and mental comfort. In the word hygge there is a certain lifestyle and practice of creating a pleasant and cozy environment that affects our well-being. Numerous statistics show that the Danes are the happiest people in the world, they have prosperity, they supposedly work 37 hours a week and have 6 we-eks of vacation. They care about the balance between professional life and leisure and family life. You can take an example from them, read about hygge and get inspired, take something for yourself from their ideas.

You can invite a few friends over (with or without children) and spend the whole Sunday together, preparing dinner together, playing with the children, playing a game or sitting carelessly on the couch. You can go with your friends to the park or meadow with a blanket and food and have a picnic. You can stay home with your family and have a plan for not scheduling your time. You can also be alone, sleep, walk around the house, read, be with yourself, create something. Or you can take out the paint, spread the sheets and newspapers on the floor and indulge in creative joy with your kids (or alone). The conditions for successful hygge, in my opinion, are as follows: you leave your pho-nes and other media, you don't drink alcohol (unless symbolically), you are together consciously and at ease, you eat something good, you do something nice, you have time. Do you like it? me very much!

When you read your dreams and you get an angel

High sensitive people usually have a lot of dreams. Their sensitivity is largely in their brain and way of thinking. Too much thinking disturbs you during the day, and dreams disturb you at night. If you're highly sensitive, you know exactly what I'm talking about. You dream a lot, you dream a lot of nonsense, a lot of things come from reality, there are also a lot of absurdities. You may have nightmares and dreams that are very real. Some are probably insignificant, a mix of everything you've seen, heard, or experienced in a day or earlier in your life. Some can be ignored, but not all.

Two days ago I had a dream that a childhood friend told me to reach out to my ancestors for support. He mentioned the woman's name, but it sounded strange: Aneida, Alenia? I knew there was a word no in the name. He was talking about some ancestor, and I thought he was talking about some ancient goddess. However, after waking up, I began to analyze this dream. Some time ago I discovered that my dreams have messages encoded with symbols and cannot be interpreted directly. I started to explore the subject and think about this name and after a while I came up with the name Aniela (she has a no inside). My great-grandmother's name was Angela. This great-grandmother did not live to see me come into the world. They told me about her and I wished I had never met her. When I see her name on my grandma's (her daughter's) grave, I think about her and how this name would be cool for my daughter. And the ancestor like a bull. But how to reach for its support? Why? I started surfing the Internet and found the meaning of the name Aniela. The name Angela comes from the Latin word angelus, which means angel and messenger. Interesting. Angela is a walking goodness. She is gentle and friendly, kind and sympathetic. It helps with the reflex of the heart. She loves nature, values freedom, gets tired in the crowd (maybe I am similar to her?). She is prudent. He thinks for a long time before making important decisions. Or did I get an Angel? Why wouldn't I think so? I might as well think I'm dreaming nonsense, but I like the version with Angela and Angel better.

In this dream, I was talking to the mother of this childhood friend about the hydrangea flower. I also read about him. Hydrangea - a symbol of honesty and gratitude. And also, a symbol of deep understanding between people, not necessarily in a romantic relationship. It can be between friends or family members. Or maybe this symbol indicates me contact with you? Maybe it's about our deep and wise understanding between women? Maybe it's about a deeper level of understanding? I like reading dreams sometimes. Interesting things come out of it, and I look for symbols in my dreams that hold messages for me. Yes, I may be crazy, but I'm fine with it.

And today, surprise - my dad (who has as fucked up dreams as me) called and said that he dreamed about me. And it's interesting that we live in dreams, and not only in our own. He said I was at his place in a red dress. Apparently, I looked very feminine and said that I would cry when I got home, not now. So how? Does he know I cry at home sometimes, and I look pretty good on top? That's true, but the fatherly care in it was very nice. And two days ago, I actually cried at home alone. Maybe he sensed?

And I immediately asked him about great-grandmother Aniela. He said that she was a good, warm and very helpful woman. She was very resourceful and hands-on. Apparently, she was involved in charity, collecting money for the Trinitarians - the Order of the Holy Trinity in Krakow. Too bad I never met her in my lifetime. Good thing I have it now though. *Great-grandmother Angel, I feel your presence and thank you for accompanying me. My angel, my guardian, you always stand by me.*

When you read Java and you get a boar

A boar came to me one day. Uninvited. Nobody expected him. If I had to choose, I would choose another animal, so pretty, dignified and associated with something nice, like strength. And here you are, the boar himself. He came to me and to my favorite friend Eliza. He appeared and introduced a funny mood that prevails between us to this day. I cannot describe this meeting here. Maybe it's not necessary. Anyway, it was funny, magical and surprising. Because sometimes in life there are daydreams. And such dreams can also be read.

Boar. *The wild boar is the only wild animal in the Polish language whose wildness has been so literally written down and emphasized in its name. So the wild boar must be no different than wild! [...] The figure/image of a wild boar, when it appears in dreams, visions, persistent associations and in strange cases, i.e. synchronicities, as well as in meetings with wild boars as such in the forest, above all, carries an appeal not to stop, not to stop half way or at the beginning. It invites you to go deeper and deeper into matters and undertakings. He calls for us to identify with these things, and not just peek at them with a cold-eyed eye. The figure of the wild calls us to live, with our whole being. It encourages you to develop what you have authentically, your own. To stop lying to yourself and deceiving others. At the same time, he admonishes that deep commitment will not be avoided, and neither will the dangers that you must face. The boar announces an authentic life, although, as if in return, not safe at all. But in the face of dangers it cries out: you will survive. The wild boar encourages self-reliance and self-reliance. He reminds you that some matters cannot be settled by handing them over to others, commissioning or buying. He says that a large and important part of life must be lived and experienced for yourself. It also reminds about practice, about the fact that "pots are not made by saints" (clay - mud - the favorite matter of wild boars!) The appearance of the wild boar must often be understood in such a way that imagining, planning and theorizing are over, it's time to get to work really[1].*

The description of the meaning of the emerging boar speaks for itself, it speaks for me, it speaks for you. This boar for me is information that I read from what appeared in reality. Yes, among other things, I read Java. And wildness is a beautiful term from the world of femininity. I believe that wildness is an amazing characteristic of every woman. Or it's just amazing to be a woman when she's wild. Wild, or what? Free, living in a natural environment, undomesticated, spontaneous, independent, strong, going her own way, living with all her heart, a bit crazy.

---

[1] *Article available online, by the date 25.01.2023. Translated to English by Maria Pogwizd* www.taraka.pL

When you see relations between men and woman

Some people say women are from Venus, and men are from Mars. Venus is the second planet from the Sun, then Earth, then Mars. Women are closer to the sun, closer to emotions and warmth. The men are a bit further away, probably a bit cooler for them. And between their worlds is Earth. So they meet halfway. Woman is from Venus and Man is from Mars. They meet each other on a new Earth, they do not know it. Everyone from their world comes. At first they are delighted with each other. They get to know each other, watch their differences with curiosity and make a nest on the beautiful Earth. Over time, it turns out that it is not easy for them. A woman craves the warmth she knows. Needs constant heating. And he? And he doesn't understand why she needs so much warmth. At first, he heats it, but then over time, he doesn't have the strength to do it anymore, or he doesn't see much sense in it. They live together on a beautiful, new planet for them and after a while they stop noticing its beauty. They begin to treat her as their own, stop admiring her. A woman ceases to be delighted with a man over time, and a man with a woman. They just live on Earth and try to make ends meet. They don't notice how beautiful it is that they are together. They go to work, give birth to children, live at home and spend little time outdoors. The differences between them become an unbearable, everyday reality and they are not so cute anymore. She complains that he doesn't understand her and doesn't give her what she needs. And he complains that she still has reservations about him, that she doesn't accept him as he is. Problems with simple communication begin. Aliens from two planets inhabiting Earth may start to fight each other over time. Complain to each other. Blame each other for your misfortune. This is a black scenario. Unfortunately, we know it well.

Venus is the second *planet from the Sun. It is sometimes called Earth's "sister" or "twin" planet as it is almost as large and has a similar composition. As an interior planet to Earth, Venus (like Mercury) appears in Earth's sky never far from the Sun, either as morning star or evening star. Aside from the Sun and Moon, Venus is the brightest natural object in Earth's sky, capable of casting visible shadows on Earth at dark conditions and being visible to the naked eye in broad daylight.*[1]

Mars is the fourth planet from the Sun and the second-smallest planet in the Solar System, only being larger than Mercury. In the English language, Mars is named for the Roman god of war. Mars is a terrestrial planet with a thin atmosphere (less than 1% that of Earth's), and has a crust primarily composed of elements similar to Earth's crust, as well as a core made of iron and nickel. Mars has surface features such as impact craters, valleys, dunes and polar ice caps. It has two small and irregularly shaped moons, Phobos and Deimos.[2]

New observations show that despite the huge difference in size and distance from the Sun, Mars and Venus are remarkably similar! Both planets have streams of electrically charged particles escaping from the planetary atmospheres. The particles are accelerated when they collide with the solar wind, which consists of electrical particles from the sun. The atmosphere of Venus is thin and dense, while Mars, on the other hand, is thin and thick. Despite this, the magnetometer showed that the structures of both magnetic fields are very similar. www.news. astronet.pl[3] *Hi hi hi…*

Venus is a Roman goddess, whose functions encompass love, beauty, desire, sex, fertility, prosperity, and victory. In Roman mythology, she was the ancestor of the Roman people through her son, Aeneas, who survived the fall of Troy and fled to Italy. Julius Caesar claimed her as his ancestor. Venus was central to many religious festivals, and was revered in Roman religion under numerous cult ti-

---

[1] A part from the article on Wikipedia, available for the day: 25.01.2023 https://en.wikipedia.org/wiki/Venus

[2] A part from the article on Wikipedia, available for the day: 25.01.2023 https://en.wikipedia.org/wiki/Mars

[3] A part from the article from, translated to English by Maria Pogwizd

tles.

In ancient Roman religion and myth, Mars was the god of war and also an agricultural guardian, a combination characteristic of early Rome. He was the son of Jupiter and Juno, and was pre-eminent among the Roman army's military gods. Most of his festivals were held in March, the month named for him (Latin Martius), and in October, which began the season for military campaigning and ended the season for farming.[1]

So we have Venus - a planet shining brightly in the sky, associated with the morning and evening, i.e. the beginning and end of the day. We have a geologically and tectonically inactive Mars, but very similar in structure to Earth. We have the Roman Gods, considered the patrons of spring. Goddess of love and god of war. How can they get along? And they met on Earth, and the longer they lived, the more unhappy they became. What can save them? I think that further self-knowledge, opening up to differences, searching for similarities, self-acceptance, love and communication. They can remind themselves every day that they met on Earth where life is possible. They met on a beautiful common Earth. They have nowhere to go back to because there is no life where they came from. They can talk to each other and tell each other about their worlds. They can create a new quality together. And although they don't really know how, they can work together, they can decide together how they want to live. They can talk about their needs: she about the warmth she longs for, he about peace and lonely journeys through the beautiful wilderness of his world. Together they can create a new quality, something that each of them could not even imagine individually. And they can be in it together to make it more fun. And they can create something good, provided that they are open, kind and honest with each other. And the prerequisite for their success is that they will cooperate with each other and that they will communicate well and clearly with each other. If they lack any of these elements, their situation can become very dangerous. They may try to destroy themselves and everything they have previously created together. They may stop wanting to be together, because they will be exhausted by such an incomplete life.

---

[1] A part of the on Wikipedia, available for the day: 25.01.2023 https://en.wikipedia.org/wiki/Mars_(mythology)

When you listen to your heart

The latest scientific discoveries show that we do not think only with our brain. We still have a heart in which there are about 40,000. sensory neurons identical in structure to those in the brain. It is as if the heart is a small brain that thinks and feels. The heart and the brain have an electromagnetic connection that sends information to each other. More information flows from the heart to the brain than vice versa. Not all information is taken seriously by the brain. This may explain the frequent inconsistency of thoughts with feelings and such strange phenomena as: unjustified emotional states, guts or intuition.

I think that through the heart we have direct contact with information important to us, but often we are not ready for this information and feelings, we do not take them seriously.

I'm having a tougher day today. It's the 20th day of the lunar cycle, my form is clearly falling and it's hard for me to think and write today. And I'll tell you, by the way, how I listen to my heart. I ignore them first, out of habit. It reprimands and shouts something. I pretend I don't hear anything. I feel internal tension, I feel uncomfortable inside myself, I like myself a little less and I start to think that something is wrong with me, but when I stop for a moment, I see signals coming from the heart. Ah, I think: it wants to tell me something. I sit comfortably and touch my heart with my hand, usually with two. I touch the middle part between the breasts, where it gets so blissful and warm. I fly away quickly, I don't think about anything for a while and when I come back to consciousness, it seems to me that I sailed away somewhere much further, as if into space. I stay in this state of pleasant suspension for a while. And then I ask. I am asking about something that is bothering me or bothering me. And the heart responds. He responds almost immediately, speaks briefly, concisely and to the point. And it often surprises me. This meeting lasts a few minutes and changes the perspective, relieves the earlier tension. Here is my last minute internal conversation:

Heart - Dear, you are so busy, it's day 20 of your writing, you have the right to feel tired.
Mind - What should I do about it?
Heart - Get a good night's sleep.

Today, for the first time, the heart started the conversation first. It surprised me a lot! I'm going to sleep well, without hesitation or remorse!
   Bye, see you tomorrow.

And as for the end, I thought of Shakespeare's sonnet:

William Shakespeare
Sonnet XLVI

Mine eye and heart are at a mortal war,
How to divide the conquest of thy sight;
Mine eye my heart thy picture's sight would bar,
My heart mine eye the freedom of that right.
My heart doth plead that thou in him dost lie,
A closet never pierced with crystal eyes,
But the defendant doth that plea deny,
And says in him thy fair appearance lies.
To 'cide this title is impannelled
A quest of thoughts, all tenants to the heart;
And by their verdict is determined
The clear eye's moiety, and the dear heart's part:
As thus: mine eye's due is thine outward part,
And my heart's right, thine inward love of heart.

When you realize you are out of this world

I have started writing this letter on the first day of the moon cycle (that's how I call my menstrual cycle, it just sounds better). I felt a great strength in myself and I really wanted to talk to you. I felt like writing the whole series. How did I know that? I have no idea, except from the heart. I sat down to write and today we are already on day 21 of the cycle. The phases of the moon flew through me. And tomorrow it's new. Now I am in the most difficult phase. I am tense, nervous, slightly crying, so delicate, I feel hungry, I swell, I take water (in my mouth too).

I thought I'd tell you how I experience my cyclicality, how I see it, how I take care of myself in different periods of the cycle. Maybe you will need such a look at yourself, at your constant change of needs.

BLOOD - a time of relief, tranquility, the need for isolation, self-focus, but also a time of creativity, excitement, new energy and new ideas. During this time, a cheerful mood returns to me, a desire to develop, a sense of the meaning of life and the desire to explore it. It was during this period that the vision of writing to you came to me and the great strength for NEW. This is the period when strength and ideas return. Tip - TAKE.

DEVELOPMENT - time of creation, time of action, time of development, growth of strength. Tip - ACT!

FERTILITY - it is a surge of a great wave of vitality, creative ideas, energy to act, joy. A time of well-being, a sense of completeness and adequacy. For me, it was Valentine's Day. The letter included topics about sex, including in my dreams. And writing was smooth and abundant (i.e. in creative fertility). Tip - TAKE IT.

TENSION - time of tension, nerves, irritation, tremors. At this time, there are some difficult situations, conflicts, anger at the injustice of this world. Because the world is unfair, I believe. There are important problems, the desire to change and improve yourself and the world. This is the time of anger energy, which can also be constructive. There was a slowdown in writing, a greater desire to rest. Tip - REST.

The set of guidelines for each described cycle time indicates a certain regularity. Take - act - be - rest. This is the lunar cycle for me. A time to take from the world, a time to give to the world, a time to be in the world and enjoy being, and a time to rest. The last time of the cycle is the hardest - allowing yourself to rest in our culture is not very popular. Time to rest and calm down (this is the turn of tension and blood). The continuation of the cycle depends on how we approach each other during this time. If you rest properly and calm down, you will probably have more strength and joy from the next stages. I already know that now I am in the most difficult time and I look at myself with a grain of salt. You want to cry - cry. You get angry - it's hard. You don't know what's wrong with you - that's okay. You don't want to go out to people - stay at home. It's Sunday - don't take off your pajamas. You're okay so fucked up. Instead of getting angry at yourself, take a book, tea and a blanket. Mute the kids or send them somewhere. Suggest a lonely walk to your husband hi hi hi .... The more I take, act, be and rest, the more satisfaction I get from ordinary everyday life, the more valuable my life seems to me.[1]

---

[1] exercise 52

When you are out of your anger

The end of tension is the time of digesting the stress accumulated earlier, it is the time of explosions. At this time, I am a volcano, inside it is buzzing, an eruption is about to happen. When I rest well and take care of myself during this time, the breakouts are smaller. However, if they happen - I try to accept myself with them. And I'm sorry for them. It gets hit by the closest ones, they're closest to the seismic areas. And here again I express my respect for men and partners - it's beautiful that you tolerate it and continue to love it!

When you are as tense as a string

Our whole life is also a cycle. The time of blood - this is the time of our birth and early childhood, the time of intensive building of what is new; time to focus and take. Development - it's growing up, maturing, time to learn and act. Fertility - this is the period of the greatest energy and joy in life. Time to give yourself to others, time for children, time for professional development, time to be.

What time do we have now? Oh! It doesn't look good. Do we have a time of tension? A time when we experience what we have collected. Time of inner tremors. Maybe there is anger at the way we live, maybe there is a desire to change ourselves and the world? This last period is definitely the time to learn how to rest properly. Time to respect yourself and take special care of yourself (so that there are as few explosions as possible). It's time to release the momentum, let go, time for yourself. It's time for you.

For me, this time turned out to be a time of increased sensitivity. Or maybe, I started to observe myself and I finally clearly noticed and understood this sensitivity in myself. Maybe the sensitivity is just as high, but I stopped agreeing to too high loads. I also know that for me less burden means more energy. Such a paradox. When I back off a little, take care of myself and rest, I have more energy and take on more meaningful activities. I guess then I can choose better and I'm more efficient. And that's it, that's it!

I am full of paradoxes. When I'm slower, I'm faster and more efficient. When I do less, I do better. When I want less, I get more. When I accept that I am weak, I become stronger. When I allow myself to be sad, I laugh beautifully afterwards. When I accept fear and act, I become brave. When I let go of perfectionism, it's easier for me to develop. The more I accept the little girl in me, the more mature I become.

When you discover how much good is around us

The best communication between your heart and mind is through a few feelings: appreciation, gratitude, care, and empathy. You can take care to cherish these feelings, you can water them in yourself so that they grow nicely inside you. When you have these moments of contact with the heart by touching and focusing on it, you can trigger them in yourself and send them to the brain. The brain in such conditions thinks better, cooperates more willingly. He gets a signal that it is safe, that there is no stress and there is no need to run away or defend yourself.

I have another task for you. I suggest you buy yourself another notebook. Again, the most beautiful in the whole universe. It will be a Notebook of Goods. In it you will write good things, situations, feelings, observations. Every night you can write down a few sentences about what good happened to you today. You can write about respect for a man, appreciation for someone, about your gratitude, you can write about the beauty of this world, about nice coincidences. It will be a book of good news, unlike what you hear and see in the media. It will be a notebook balancing the reality in you. If at the same time you slightly reduce the influx of unpleasant information about the world to you (Internet, TV, news on the radio), the balance will be easier.

Write about the fact that someone smiled at you, that you saw a nice plant on your way to work, that the wind was so warm today that the sun gave a nice light in the evening. Write about your husband's beautiful eyes, about your children's play, which also put you in a good mood. Write about your calm breathing, small successes of your own, for example, that you politely told someone no, that you said yes to yourself. Write about memories, dreams, how the book you read smells, about the light of candles in the cemetery, about your interesting creative ideas. Write about the feeling of peace that appeared in you out of nowhere and was with you for a few minutes. Write about meeting a nice lady in the doctor's waiting room, about a song that caused emotion. Write about tea with a friend, cashew mayonnaise and the taste of whole meal bread with avocado paste.

And on the first pages of this notebook, write some kind words addressed to yourself and about yourself. When you have written down the entire notebook, celebrate and, for example, organize a hygge meeting at your home. Or buy yourself beautiful flowers or your dream perfume. And read randomly selected notes to your loved ones.

When you realize you are beautiful

Despite the time in which the body changes into an older one, what we have inside remains unchanged. Other people probably see you differently than you do. Would you like to know what they really think about you? It seems to me that your loved ones are more kind to you than you are yourself. You too are probably more accepting of others than of yourself. Let's check it. Ask 10 people who are important to you to write a list of the qualities they see in you. Tell them to write what they think of you, honestly. Let them write what they want. Write down the good things you read in your good notebook. Accept them and don't argue with them. Also write what you think about yourself. After reading this letter, maybe it will be easier for you to do it with self-love or at least with sympathy .[1]

Cultivate your inner beauty. The external will pass away and matter less. Do you remember any elderly person in your life, some wrinkled, wonderful grandma? Beloved grandfather? Do you remember their inner beauty? Did their wrinkles matter to you? Maybe you haven't even seen them much? Think about how beautiful some older people are. Think about how beautiful some unbeautiful women are. Describe each meeting with a beautiful person in your notebook. It doesn't matter if you're older or younger.[2]

---

[1] exercise 53
[2] exercise 54

When you realize you can make it

My dear reader. Today is the New Moon. Another important one. I don't know much about astrology, but I can feel its importance. The new moon is great in me. And although it is windy today, although I have sadness in my heart and I cried again today, I believe that I will manage. Well, what would it look like if I couldn't handle it? It's always somehow. Always after trouble comes another day and does not ask: is it possible? Today I had a difficult situation with a leaking roof and felt the lack of a man. So I had more lessons in asking for help. Because there are men in this world. Some people have to pay for help, because they are professionals, but some will help, just from the heart, for chocolates. There is always a friend's husband, another friend's husband, another friend's husband, a colleague, an acquaintance, a neighbor. Thank you men for helping me hang lamps, move furniture, fix cupboards in the kitchen. And we installed the blinds ourselves, me and my favorite friend Agnieszka. And asking for help is not easy for me. Not for you either? It can be trained. It gets easier over time. So you can be alone, but not necessarily on your own, because there's always someone nice if you ask, of course. Asking for help is a sign of strength, not weakness. And besides, do you remember that you are not alone because you have yourself?

And the new moon brings new ones. I opened a page on Facebook – *Feminine Space (today Sikorka Flow)*. I felt it was a good idea to finally go out into a wider space, to the women of the world. I can try to speak from the privacy of the therapeutic office to the world of women differently, wider and braver. It's not easy for me, such a breakthrough, but since I've already started writing to you, I've already made a big step. The next ones will just be a continuation of this.

And Feminine Space is a name that has been walking with me for over 10 years - this is the name of all my workshops for women. The spaces beautifully define the multidimensionality of female nature. We have many. Writing to you, I noticed that I write about many very different things, I move in different spaces (yours and mine), spaces of broadly understood femininity.

Today, I came home and I was touched that I have a house, a roof over my head and a warmly decorated space. After returning from this windy and rainy world, I can take refuge in my cozy little space. Spontaneous tears of happiness and gratitude flowed down my cheeks.

I still have financial fears, but they don't last long either, because either some new job appears, some new circumstance, or new ideas, somehow magically enough for me. I thank the world for its cooperation in this field. And I wish that for you too. I believe that a woman is just as efficient as a man and in our world she can earn her own money. I wish you peace and development in this matter.

Maybe you don't intend to leave your partner, maybe you're fine where you are. If so, that's beautiful. Kiss my partner for me. Maybe you have other challenges and you are afraid of whether you can handle it? You know, you'll never know if you don't try.

When you start liking your open mind

I love being sober. I like being aware, I like a clear mind, clarity of thinking, simplicity of perception. Some people think it's my professional perversion because I've been an addiction therapist for many years. but no. I feel very sorry for them (addicts) that they destroy their mind, that they do not like transparency and truth in themselves.

And I wanted to tell you to be careful, because in such a difficult time, you can quickly get lost. With drugs, it's like these men with cookies, they only work for a while. Then the gray reality returns. Or it may come back with more negative force, after the temporary relief you give yourself. I do not recommend. And I know many fantastic addicted women who became addicted at this later age and a slightly more difficult time for themselves. And they are fantastic because they heal and become more themselves because they are closer to the clarity of their own mind.

And, please, don't drink alcohol when the kids fall asleep, don't drink in the evening when you've done everything at home, don't drink as a reward, don't drink to cry, don't drink with yourself! And if you do drink, drink symbolically. Be the mistress of your head.

Some anger won't hurt your beauty

It got me! Today I'm pissed off. I'm shaking inside. And there aren't even great reasons. You can just get angry! Together with you I go through my cycle and reach the most difficult moment. You know it, right? And how can you live with yourself? How will anyone close to you cope? Surely there are ways to ease the situation. You can talk about your mood, about the causes of anger. You can reveal what is happening to you. Call your friend and tell her how she tugs at you inside, name it. You can also write various nonsense from your head into a notebook. The first one, of course. Even bad words.

Anger is an amazing energy. It is used for defense, for rebellion, it can also be used for development. We learned in childhood that the anger of beauty is harmful. Is it? More nonsense. Maybe when she feels it, she's not very nice to look at. A woman who knows how to get angry is more beautiful. At least internally. For me, such women are difficult, who do not get angry, who are always kind, obliging. They are a bit boring and dangerous. I prefer to stay away from those. I feel anxious and sad about them.

Today, my tension at the end of the day was relieved by laughing on the phone with my wild friend. I was crying with laughter. And everything let go. And the light mood returned.

And these teachings about good girls, about the fact that it is not appropriate, that it is not appropriate, what people will say, that girls should not get angry - today we put these teachings deep somewhere. Cholera! Baba is only supposed to cry, be weak and quiet, right? Why should a girl be polite? So that she will grow up to be a good, loving and obliging beef ass? Oh no!

Describe one example from your life when your anger was very useful to you. Me, when I once fucked a friend from elementary school in the head, he definitely stopped bothering me. I am proud of it to this day. A woman who can get angry is less comfortable, but she is more genuine. You're either a beef ass or an authentic woman, the choice is yours. ;-)

And if you don't like what I write, I invite you to a workshop for good girls entitled I can handle myself. We will train politeness to be in the strong part of the head. The workshops will take place soon in The Sadness Valley, at the community center at Polish Mothers 11 street. You will be able to learn more about how to make yourself feel guilty, how to deny unnecessary spontaneity, how to act in life so that everyone will like it and how to make us more interested in what others say about us and think. There will also be exercises on how to react joyfully to violence, how to deceive a partner in active addiction and keep him at home so that he does not go to friends. The program also includes other topics: how to choose friends who gossip a lot and willingly talk badly about us behind our backs, how to change a partner for the worse, how to drive yourself to death cleaning and empty your guts. Plus, you'll learn risk-taking techniques to protect your partner from women's anger, and how to discipline your kids to lie on the couch with their feet up while you mop the floor so they don't soil it. And in the free technique of efficient lamenting over yourself, complaining about your fate and ways to accept a hopeless situation as it is. The cost of the workshop is only $8, which is how much you have left for your needs per year. I invite you. [1]

---

[1] exercise 55

When it turns out he can't give it to you

Unfortunately, I fell into the same trap that many women fall into. I wanted my man to heal me of my pain, satisfy my longings, read my mind and fulfill my desires. I felt a huge hunger for love and attention with him. I wanted it to confirm my worth and to convince me that I am amazing and beautiful. I was loved, but I didn't feel love. I wanted him to be a good husband, and I turned out to be a bad wife. I left and felt abandoned. I wanted too much from him. I just couldn't love. I got burned on my expectations.

Today I see that I wanted from him what he could not give me. I'm also sorry I wasn't better for him. I found a different path to myself and my needs. I found my way back to myself and gave myself a lot of what I wanted from him. Do you understand me? I don't really believe it myself, but I've had a great peace of mind for some time now. And I have something else. I don't know if I can describe it in words, but I'll try.

I have serenity, I have lightness inside and no waiting. The state of not waiting is simply being. I'm not even looking forward to tomorrow. It's today and I focus on what I have to do, I work with my whole being, I listen to people, also with my whole being, I clean completely absorbed in cleaning, I hang the laundry and I feel that I am. Now. I don't need anything and everything is fine. Well, I admit it's not like that all the time, but it's a huge percentage of my life right now. A huge difference between what I had, for example, a year ago. Then I had a constant pain inside me, an invisible sense of missing and longing for something (yesterday or tomorrow). I kept crying. My eyes were so wet, sometimes I didn't even know why I was crying. My soul cried. Before, I was always chasing something, and now I feel like I've finally caught up. I've caught up with myself. It's an amazing feeling to have yourself like this. It's such a beautiful feeling that I dare say I've never felt like this before. It is such a state and such a feeling that everything is in its place, that it is as it should be. And the extra free from the world is that it protects me. As if as a reward. I feel fully taken care of by the universe. She says to me: you're safe and you'll be fine. You're not alone.

When you are

If you've read the letter this far, you've probably seen many similarities to me in yourself. Probably something I wrote spoke to you. So if you're like me, it's possible that you're a strong and sensitive woman at the same time. You have layers of wildness in you that want to get out of you and maybe you even have a little more desire to reveal it to the world. You may also be brave. You know, the thing about courage is that you may not know how much you have until you use it. And you can say that you are afraid, that you never dared, that you were always afraid to explore new things. Know that despite fear, you can act. And that is real courage. Action despite fear. What is the art of being brave and not being afraid? Understand? I also know that you are an independent person and you can decide about your life. You can follow your own path in life. Well, who's going to stop you? You have a life and you can use it to live it your way. Or, of course, you can do nothing, change nothing, and live as you have lived. From now on, you have a complete ban on whining and complaining. Because it will also be your choice. Accepting and appreciating what you have can be a great idea for you, but remember, no whining! Don't waste energy, just live.

Maybe after reading my words nothing will change for you. If you don't take any steps yourself, reading me won't change anything for you, that's for sure. Now you have a lot of inspiration, ideas and tasks that you can do at a later, more appropriate time. Do it your way, but do something! It won't do itself. And you will reach the apogee of your own development if you reach such a calm thought in yourself that it's nice that you are not young anymore.

When you are grateful you are not so young anymore

Seriously, that's cool. I'm happy there! I'm also glad I'm not older. I'm just like that. I don't have to go back to school anymore, I don't get tired of my peers, teachers don't stress me out, I don't have to get up at eight every day (completely pointless). I've already given birth to children, so I'm pregnant. Big these children, more and more independent. The Beauty Age Crisis is over. I am getting smarter and more relaxed. I wouldn't want to back down anymore.

And now I will offer you an interesting meeting with a person 10 years older than you. This will be your meeting with yourself. Imagine yourself in 10 years. What will you look like, what will you wear, what will you do? Write a letter from your older self to yourself right now. Do not think too much. Just sit down and write spontaneously. I wonder what the old one will tell you.

I want to tell you that you can work to stay young longer, stay fit longer. You can influence whether you will age quickly or slowly. The exercise of heart contact, which I wrote about in the chapter on listening to your heart, is the activation of immune protection processes and life-promoting chemicals. When we send the optimal signal from our heart to the brain, it is strengthened, healed and calmed. The brain receives a signal that it is safe and knows that it does not have to fight or run away. In the so-called coherence of the heart, anti-aging hormones (dehydroepiandrosterone - DHEA[1]), because there is room for it. Under stress, these hormones take a backseat to more life-threatening signals.

Yesterday, just before going to sleep, in this state of heart, I asked

---

[1] Read more about DHEA on https://en.wikipedia.org/wiki/ Dehydroepiandrosterone

myself: What should I say to her (i.e. to you)? And I got an immediate response: Tell her you love her. Amazing, right? How can I tell you that I love you? I don't know you at all, but believe it or not, I felt this love very strongly. And the mind would like to quarrel with the heart here, but why? I won't give him that opportunity. I turn off my mind and say to you: I don't know you, but I feel that I love you! It may not be love in a standard, colloquial form, but such love straight from the heart... So simple and pure. And I want to tell you that I love myself very much. It's hard for me to admit it, but it's the truth. And I wish you such self-love.

I believe (because I am a believer) that you can influence your life, that you have the tools available for this (e.g. heart). You can make you stay young longer. I also believe that the language of the human heart can heal the separation that has led you to the crisis you are in.

And when looking in the mirror, do not look at the details (wrinkles, sagging, lack of firmness). Look at the man you see, look into your eyes. Look at the person you are. See the whole thing. Other people also look at your wholeness, they don't see the details that you cling to. They see you. And they are more interested in who you are, how you behave, what you say, than the details of your face - I'm sure of it. Is it logical?

And actually it depends on you whether you will see an old wrinkled woman in the mirror or maybe an interesting world, internally beautiful and unique person.[1]

---

[1] exercise 56

When the life happens to be the best teacher

I have learned a lot about myself lately. I have experienced a lot and matured a bit. I like myself more and get along better with myself. Life teaches. I think this crisis of mine was very necessary for me. Now that I see it, it made a lot of sense. I hope this crisis has helped you too. Without him, I'd be where I was, and it wasn't fun there. Without him, I would not have understood many human dramas in depth. I wouldn't have written this book without him. Without him, I would not have developed and used my courage. The glass that was between me and the world shattered. I was unknowingly disconnecting myself from reality. The glass hurt me a bit in the crash of the shatter, but now I'm healing my wounds and nothing stands between me and what is beautiful. The blood has already washed away, the wounds are healed, I'm still a little sore, but I can live on.

I've never been so close to myself. I've never felt so calm before. I haven't laughed so much in a long time, I haven't danced so much in a long time, I haven't slept so well in a long time. It's been a long time since I wanted so little, I haven't given up so much for a long time, I haven't been so taken care of for a long time.

And here I think of the goddess Psyche - the personification of the human soul, presented as a young girl with butterfly wings. Psyche was a symbol of the immortal soul. The second meaning of the name Psyche, meaning a butterfly, refers to folklore, where the souls of the dead were sometimes depicted in this way. After the unfortunate night, when Psyche, persuaded by her sisters, checked her husband's appearance and scalded him with hot oil, the girl was distraught. When the goddess of love found Psyche, she immediately began punishing her. She decided that she would give the girl such hard and impossible work that she would still have an excuse to prolong the sentence inde-

finitely. Psyche was an earthly princess who, by performing many difficult tasks, in the name of love, eventually became a goddess on Olympus. Psyche[1] made mistakes and life was not kind to her. Despite this, she did not give up and went forward, she was very brave, although she often thought about taking her own life.

---

[1] More about Psyche on https://en.wikipedia.org/wiki/Psyche_ (mythology)

When you wonder what will you leave behind?

Now I know that I want to leave a nice impression. I want to be a warm memory in the thoughts of my loved ones. I want to be a support for others, even when I'm gone. I want them to feel that I have loved and to feel that I still love. I want them to know that I managed to live my life well and that I managed to enjoy it to the fullest. I want them to remember my smiling face, to hear my contagious laugh, to make their hearts lighten at the thought of me, not heavy. And to do that, I already know what to do.

I'm not turned on by the image of an overworked unhappy woman. I don't think it turns anyone on.

And then lived a short and happy life

Maybe I'll live a short life, because I'm not so young anymore, but it's important that I live sensibly and happily. And yesterday I had an interesting difficult experience. I felt very bad. I had these symptoms and it felt like I was about to have a stroke. I know it and I know the symptoms. I've had three pre-strokes like this in my life. Or was it micro strokes? Well, unfortunately, I don't know, because I didn't check it then. I don't like hospitals and I was afraid of medical intervention. Yesterday I felt like I could disappear from this world in the blink of an eye. I thought I might not be here for a while. From this perspective, I looked at myself and my problems and my thinking cleared up a bit. I am very grateful today that I am alive. I used the heart exercise and drifted off into space for a few moments, and it calmed me down a lot. Who knows, maybe I even lowered my blood pressure? All symptoms subsided, but I took today off work to rest. I've had some stress recently, they accumulated in a few days, they like it so much, they gather and perform willingly in groups or at least in pairs. My body was overloaded and couldn't handle the stress. I need rest. These are signals coming from within me. I'm not that young anymore, I should take more care of myself. And I promise myself and you that I will go to the doctor and have my head examined. Nobody does this preventively, we always wait for serious problems before we go for a head examination. Or maybe you have something to test? Are you procrastinating on something? If you do not want something in you to develop without your knowledge, then do some research, calm your heart, or start treatment if necessary.

If I can die at any time, then as long as I live, I can live at any time. Oh, how wisely I said!

And I know it won't be perfect. There will be eternal happiness and peace. I know there will be troubles and problems. I know I will cry sometimes. I know I can go on with my life, and perhaps a little more than I used to, I know how to do it.

Last Saturday I cried thinking about me and my husband, about our drama, remembering the good times. The tears wouldn't stop. I allowed myself these tears. This Sunday brought a lot of joy. First I cleaned, then we were visited by two large and two small women. We spent time hygging carefree and joyful. I go to bed with a clean floor and clean thoughts. Ah, life. :-)

The end of the letter

After I wrote this sentence: Ah life and I was thinking what else to write, I went to the toilet. And here's a surprise. Another moon cycle has just started for me. There's nothing like contact with the moon in the bathroom. And I already knew that this was such an unusual end to this letter to you. :-) [1]

If you want to respond to my letter:
    sikorka.flow@gmail.com

If you would like to see me and listen to me – feel free to visit my YouTube channel:
    Sikorka Flow: https://youtube.com/c/SikorkaFlow

If you would like to purchase my other items, please visit Amazon.

Eve Sikora

---

[1] exercise 57 and 58

Afternote

When you get a mid-life crisis…
https://en.wikipedia.org/wiki/Crisis
https://opoka.org.pl/biblioteka/T/TS/wam_2012_pokonaj_ kryzys_02.html

When you are writing your life scenario
https://www.gallup.com/cliftonstrengths/en/home.aspx

When you read Java and get a boar
www.taraka.pl

When you see relations between men and women
https://en.wikipedia.org/wiki/Mars
https://en.wikipedia.org/wiki/Wenus
www.news.astronet.pl
https://en.wikipedia.org/wiki/Mars_(mythology)

Kiedy jesteś wdzięczna, że już nie jesteś młoda
https://en.wikipedia.org/wiki/Dehydroepiandrosteron

Acknowledgments

I sincerely thank you with all my heart for your support and participation in the crisis, for the inspiration for a new life and for writing this book:

For women that are close to my heart:

Adze, Agnieszce, Agnieszce, Ani, Ani, Ani, Ani, Asi, Asi, Asi, Danusi, Darii, Dominice, Dominice, Dorotce, Dziewance, Edytce, Elizie, Ewie, Ewie, Małgosi, Ifci. Inie, Julicie, Justynce, Kamili, siostrze Kasi, Kindze, Magdzie, Magdzie, Martuszce, Marii, Marysi, Marzenie, Milenie, Moni, Natalii, Nataszce, mamie Tereni, Wiesi, Violi, babci Zosi

I put you in alphabetical order, because it was impossible to do it any other way ;-) You listened to me many times, patiently and without judging, I felt wrapped in a blanket of love next to you and accepted completely as I am - it's a great gift to have and feel you, and to use your feminine wisdom. Some of you have been further away in my life recently, but you are very close in my memories and in my heart.

For men that are important and close to my heart:

My dad Janusz, Pawłowi, Filipowi, Nikosiowi, Julkowi, Danemu, Michałowi, Edwinowi, Maćkowi, Markowi, Suchemu, Olafowi, Piotrowi, Stefanowi, Patrykowi, Maćkowi, Colinowi, Danielowi, Danielowi, Rysiowi, Maćkowi, Grzegorzowi

A supported women and men during my crisis:

Alicji, Ani, Ani, Basi, Beacie, Bogdanowi, Dominice, Grażynce, Iwonie, Irence, Justynce, Kasi, Leszkowi, Magdzie, Magdzie, Małgorzacie, Marysi, Marzenie, Natalii, Natalii, Oli, Paulinie, Rafałowi, Sybilli
You were with me during the crisis without knowing it, but you gave me a lot of support and inspiration unknowingly. It is very possible that you will find scraps of our conversations here. Your work and courage gave me strength. I wish you perseverance in following your own path in life.

Also I want to thank:

– The man of my previous life, for great love, beautiful time together, patience and amazing fatherhood
– Eliza, for support by working with the One Brain method
– beloved grandma Zosia, for great support from another world
– Mrs. Ania, for therapy sessions
– Doctor Ewa Dąbrowska, for the fruit and vegetable diet
– Circle of Women from our area (to all wise women who open their beautiful and sensitive hearts to the circle)
– Addiction Treatment Center Radzimowice in Szklarska Poręba for 17 years of cooperation, learning and professional experience – I recommend this place for addiction therapy
– Colleagues from the Addiction Treatment Clinic at the MSW Hospital in Jelenia Góra for their great kindness and great working atmosphere
– to all women who have ever worked with me, individually and during my workshops "Women's Spaces" (in Jelenia Góra, Wrocław, on Skype, in the center in Szklarska Poręba and in Skarżysko-Kamienna at the Sobriety Association Kamienna). Thank you for trusting and opening your true self, delicate spheres, painful matters, for feminine charm, for touching moments and for happy moments. It was a great pleasure for me to be with you and accompany you in your development. It is thanks to you that I am who I am. It is thanks to you and my close women that I wrote this book.
– Basia and Jacek Rydlewski and Magda Beszła, for the school of psychotherapy, acceptance, amazing atmosphere, own therapy and supervision
– Zosia Sobolewska, for therapy a long time ago in Warsaw
- Karolina and Jarek for a beautiful place for an office and a fantastic atmosphere at work
– Beauty women who nurture and add youth to various parts of my body (Edytka, Mrs. Kasia, Beatka, Milenka)
– Mother Earth and Father Universe, thank you for a beautiful house!
– To the moon, for light and signs
– To God, for love and existence

I also need to thank people from the Internet and other media:

– Academy of Children's Photography – for a beautiful time together and an amazing community of women wonderfully photographing our reality and our children
– Aurora from Norway for wonderful music and singing,
– Barbara Jurga and Ba-ha-art for all her and her wisdom,
– Comie for the album First Out of Darkness (which helped me get out of my darkness),
– Imagine Dragons for the song and music video Bad Liar,
– Jurek Owsiak for his huge heart and integration of Poles for a good cause (a bit unrelated, but I am deeply moved by the strength and goodness of this man),
– Kari Amirian for amazing music and a short personal meeting after the concert in Łódź,
– Lao Che, for intellectual nourishment and original conversations with my sons while listening to their music, about God, man and society,
– Marek Jankowski – the author of the Mała Wielka Firma podcast for inspiration in business and not only, and for what a cordial man he is,
– Metallica for an excellent concert in Krakow in 2018,
– Michał Szafrański for thinking about finances, for trust as a new currency and for who he is, crossing borders and creating a new reality for us, not only in the sphere of finance,
– Katarzyna Miller for all the books, feminine strength and wisdom,
– Okuniewska from Reykjavik for beautiful madness, courage and authenticity,
– Creators of the documentary series Strange Planet Earth,
– Wild woman – Anna Rogowska for her energy and meetings with wonderful women,
– Gregg Braden, for his lectures and unpopular knowledge
– Trójka (currently Radio Nowy Świat) – Polish Radio for music and atmosphere!

Special thanks to Limitless Mind Publishing for their work on publishing this book. Thank you: Asia, Kasia, Pati, Wojtek, Iza, Beatka, Ania and Mariusz. We met with Asia Sosnówka (so two titmouses met) in magical circumstances and our cooperation was beautiful. It was and is an amazing adventure. Thank you for your patience and wise corrections.

Big acknowledgment to the authors of the books:

Which I have read and recommend to others, which I used during my crisis and writing this book. What I wrote is mixed with what I read in many books, found on the web, overheard in conversations. I apologize if I used someone else's words without quoting them exactly. I had no head to embrace this topic from the scientific or substantive side. I hope no one is offended that they got mixed up in my head like this. Here are my readings for you, my inspirations, my support, read by me in that order:

- A ja, żem jej powiedziała – Katarzyna Nosowska
- Aspergirls – Rudy Simone
- Chcę być kochana, tak jak chcę – Katarzyna Miller
- The 5 love languages – Greg McKeown
- The highly sensitive person – Elaine Aron
- Życiologia – Miłosz Brzeziński
- Your second life starts when you realize you only have one – Raphaelle Giordano
- The highly sensitive person in love – Elaine Aron
- The life-changing magic of tidying up – Marie Kondo
- When things fell apart. A heart advice for difficult times – Pema Chodron
- Życie jest fajne – Katarzyna Miller i Małgorzata Szcześniak
- Big Magic – Elizabeth Gilbert
- Tęsknota silnej kobiety za silnym mężczyzną – Maja Storch
- Why does this keep happening to me? – Alan Downs
- Deep work – Cal Newport
- Good body – Eve Ensler
- Ona ma siłę – Iwona Wiśniewska
- I think too much – Christel Petitcollin
- Start where you are – Pema Chodron
- Mężczyzna pozwala kochać. Głód kobiety – Wilfried Wieck
- Godness in everywoman – Jean S. Bolen
- The art of living – Bob Proctor
- The rich life – Beau Henderson
- Rising Strong – Brene Brown
- Rich dad, poor dad – Robert Kiyosaki
- Dieta warzywno–owocowa dr Ewy Dąbrowskiej – Beata Anna Dą-

browska
– Holistyczne podejście do życia – Grzegorz Cieślik
– Stanowczo, łagodnie, bez lęku – Maria Król-Fijewska
– Jak się nie rozstać, a jeśli rozstać, to jak? – Katarzyna Miller and Su-
zan Giżewska
– Families and how to survive them – Robin Skynner and John Cleese
– Unconditional love – John Powell
– The gifts of imperfection – Brene Brown
– Highly sensitive people – Ilse Sand
– Być parą i nie zwariować – Katarzyna Miller and Andrzej Gryżewski

(I also read, in the meantime, some youth literature, which is a total relaxation for me, e.g. Susanne Collins, and some other books, e.g. business or photography, which I have not listed here because they are off
topic)

I will also list off things I've read once and really liked:

– Women who run with wolves – Clarissa P. Estes
– Czerwony namiot – Anita Diamant
– L'art de la simplicité – Dominique Loreau
– Kup kochance męża kwiaty – Katarzyna Miller
– Bajka to życie albo z jakiej bajki jesteś – Wojciech Eichelberger and
Agnieszka Suchowierska
– Siedem boskich pomyłek – Wojciech Eichelberger
– Kobieta bez winy i wstydu – Wojciech Eichelberger
– Seksownik, czyli mądrze i pikantnie – Katarzyna Miller and Beata
Pawłowicz
– Home Coming – John Bradshaw
– Hygge. The Danish art to happiness – Marie T. Soderberg

And I also want to thank myself:

Not that I put myself at the deep end. I've been the first for myself for a while now and I'm starting not to be ashamed of it. Thank you, Eve, for being with me from the very beginning, for friendship, for love. For our time together on this Earth. It wasn't easy for us, but we are together and together we create our beautiful inner world. Thank you for making a little girl's dream come true and becoming a psychologist. You didn't know what it was called then. Then you felt that you understood people and that you had an amazing gift of listening to others and getting to the deep level of their problems and affairs. You knew this was your life path. Thank you for finally starting to listen to yourself and your intuition. Thank you for the amazing time spent creating this book. You are an amazing person. I love you and I would like to grow with you and then grow old.

Printed in the USA
CPSIA information can be obtained
at www.ICGtesting.com
CBHW071327061224
18488CB00014B/744